the last

Mill on liberty:
a defence

International Library of Philosophy

Editor: Ted Honderich

A catalogue of books already published in the
International Library of Philosophy
will be found at the end of this volume

Mill on liberty: a defence

John Gray

Fellow of Jesus College, Oxford

ROUTLEDGE & KEGAN PAUL

London, Boston, Melbourne and Henley

First published in 1983
by Routledge & Kegan Paul Plc
39 Store Street, London WC1E 7DD,
9 Park Street, Boston, Mass. 02108, USA,
296 Beaconsfield Parade, Middle Park,
Melbourne, 3206, Australia, and
Broadway House, Newtown Road,
Henley-on-Thames, Oxon RG9 1EN
Set in Press Roman by Columns
and printed in Great Britain by
The Thetford Press Limited, Thetford, Norfolk

Library of Congress Cataloging in Publication Data

Gray, John, 1948-

Mill on liberty.
(International library of philosophy)
Includes bibliographical references and index.
1. Mill, John Stuart, 1806-1873. On liberty.
2. Liberty. I. title. II. Series.
JC585.M75G72 1982   323.44   82-16151

ISBN 0-7100-9270-9

For Marie

CONTENTS

Contents

ACKNOWLEDGMENTS AND BIBLIOGRAPHICAL NOTE

A good many people have helped me in writing this short book. It was conceived during the years in which my doctoral research on liberalism was supervised by the late John Plamenatz. Without the kindly interest John Plamenatz showed in my earliest work, and the encouragement and support I was given by my subsequent supervisors, Alan Ryan and Steven Lukes, it is doubtful that I could have ever brought the book to birth. Christopher Kirwan, my Tutor in Philosophy when I was an undergraduate at Exeter College, Oxford, has from an early stage and throughout the project's development given me valuable comment and advice on a series of drafts. The late John Rees was generous in giving me his written and spoken comments on early drafts of the book. Graeme Duncan read an early draft and was very helpful in enabling me to express myself more clearly. Sir Isaiah Berlin, who gave me extraordinarily probing and very detailed comments on a late draft, and H.L.A. Hart, whose criticisms stirred my thoughts at several stages in the book's composition, are to be thanked for their important contributions to the book's development. I owe a special debt of gratitude to Ted Honderich, who has commented on several drafts and whose criticism and encouragement have been of great value to me throughout the book's gestation. I wish to thank the Principal and Fellows of my College for granting me a period of sabbatical leave in which I was able to make considerable headway with the book.

Several people have been kind enough to read and comment on the book in its later stages. Among them I would like to thank particularly Brian Barry, Fred Berger, J.P. Day, David Gordon, D.N. MacCormick, J. Raz, D.A. Rees, A.K. Sen, C.L. Ten and W.L. Weinstein. Since no one who has read the book agrees with all of it, and since I have some-times stuck to my views against the criticisms of those who have commented on it, it is important to underline the usual disclaimer that I alone bear responsibility for the arguments advanced here.

An early version of my argument about J.S. Mill appeared as a paper entitled 'J.S. Mill on liberty, utility and rights'. Portions of that paper are reprinted by permission of New York University Press from *Human Rights* (*Nomos XXIII*), edited by J. Roland Pennock and John W. Chapman. Copyright © 1981 by New York University. I am most grate-ful to Professor Roland Pennock and to the New York University Press for granting me permission to make use of my contribution to *Nomos XXIII: Human Rights*.

My greatest debt is to my wife, to whom I have dedicated this volume.

J.N. Gray
Jesus College, Oxford

BIBLIOGRAPHICAL NOTE

The definitive edition of Mill's writings is *The Collected Works of John Stuart Mill*, Toronto University Press, 1963-. I have tried, however, always to cite the most easily available and widely used editions, e.g. the Everyman edition of *Utilitarianism, On Liberty and Representative Government*, London, Dent 1972, and in some cases, where there are very many editions of the work, I have given references to its chapter and section. A list of the sources for recent interpretations of J.S. Mill on liberty and utility is found in note 17 to chapter 1 of this book.

PREFACE

In this book a received view is contested as to the character of John Stuart Mill's writings about liberty. It has become a commonplace of the intellectual history of nineteenth-century England that the younger Mill is at best a transitional thinker whose writings on social and political questions disclose no coherent doctrine or pattern of argument, but only the efforts at synthesis of an ultimately unsuccessful eclecticism. As for *On Liberty*, it has long been the conventional view that there Mill sets out to square the circle – to give a utilitarian defence of the priority of liberty over other values. What intellectual enterprise could be more misconceived, or more clearly doomed to failure?

My aim in this study is to show by textual analysis and the reconstruction of Mill's argument that *On Liberty* is not the folly that over a century of unsympathetic critics and interpreters have represented it as being, but rather the most important passage in a train of argument about liberty, utility and rights which Mill sustained over a number of his most weighty moral and political writings. Far from being the monument to Mill's inconsistency that his critics have caricatured, *On Liberty* is consistent almost to a fault, both in its own terms and in terms of a pattern of reasoning developed in Mill's other writings in which a utilitarian theory of conduct is applied to many questions in moral and political life. *On Liberty* contains a fragment of what I call Mill's Doctrine of Liberty, in which a defence is given in utilitarian terms of the institution of a system of moral rights within which the right to liberty is accorded priority.

It is in his presentation of a utilitarian theory of justice and of moral rights, and his defence of the paramount importance of the right to liberty, that Mill's greatest originality still lies. The conception of a utilitarian theory of justice and moral rights remains a stumbling block to most contemporary moral philosophers, who are prone to consider its advocacy a symptom of confusion in thought even if it is not plainly a contradiction in terms. My submission is that this resistance to the idea of a utilitarian defence of justice and rights depends on a thin and narrow conception of Utilitarianism itself and neglects some of the most distinctive features of Mill's contribution to the utilitarian tradition. We find in J.S.Mill, I shall argue, a distinctive and powerful species of indirect utilitarianism, which lacks most of the failings rightly attributed to other forms of utilitarianism, and which is capable of generating a coherent and plausible theory of justice and of the moral right to liberty.

In the context of his writings on liberty, Mill emerges as a formidable and systematic thinker, still very much a part of the British utilitarian tradition. His Doctrine of Liberty remains open to criticism, just as it was when first he developed it. But the most salient criticisms are not those which take for granted the impossibility of a utilitarian theory of moral rights, nor those which trade on the obsolescent image of Mill as a man of half-formed ideas, caught helpless between loyalty to the utilitarian tradition and his liberal commitments. Instead, the most pertinent criticisms of Mill's defence of liberty focus on the claim that he underestimates the extent to which the various conditions and ingredients of human happiness may come into practical competition with each other, so that he fails to confront the true depth and difficulty of many real moral dilemmas. It is no part of my argument that Mill's writings contain any satisfactory response to criticisms of this latter sort, but I aim to show that much of Mill's doctrine of liberty retains force and importance even if the validity of such criticisms be conceded. This book will have served its purpose if, in presenting Mill as a systematic thinker and *On Liberty* as the expression of a coherent doctrine, it helps Mill's readers to assess his argument in a way that does justice to his intentions and his achievements.

For the man devoted to liberty, there is nothing which *makes* liberty important. And he has no reason for his devotion.

R. Rhees, *Without Answers*, London,
Routledge & Kegan Paul, 1969, p. 84.

Having said that individuality is the same thing with development, and that it is only the cultivation of individuality which produces, or can produce, well-developed human beings, I might here close the argument: for what more or better can be said of any condition of human affairs than that it brings human beings nearer to the best thing they can be? or what worse can be said of any obstruction to good than that it prevents this? Doubtless, however, these considerations will not suffice to convince those who most need convincing; and it is necessary further to show that these developed human beings are of some use to the undeveloped — to point out to those who do not desire liberty, and would not avail themselves of it, that they may be in some intelligible manner rewarded for allowing other people to make use of it without hindrance.

J.S. Mill, *On Liberty*, London, Dent
1972, pp. 121-2.

I

MILL'S PROBLEM IN
ON LIBERTY

1 A TRADITIONAL INTERPRETATION

According to a traditional view, Mill's problem in *On Liberty* is insoluble. Mill affirms that his aim there is to defend a single principle regulating interference with individual freedom of thought and action: 'One very simple principle' as he famously puts it 'as entitled to govern absolutely the dealings of society with the individual in the way of compulsion and control'.[1] His description of the principle which he seeks to defend as 'entitled to govern absolutely' the liberty-limiting interferences of state and society with individual activity suggests that Mill intends the principle to be applicable exceptionlessly in all societies save those covered by his clause excluding 'those backward states of society in which the race itself may be considered as in its nonage'.[2] In specifying the sorts of argument which he will adduce in justification of assent to his principle, Mill declares that they will appeal only to utilitarian considerations: 'It is proper to state that I forgo any advantage which could be derived to my argument from the idea of abstract right, as a thing independent of utility.'[3] Those who uphold this received view are in no doubt that the enterprise to which Mill commits himself in these statements is so misconceived as to be virtually incoherent.

Within the powerful current of destructive criticism of Mill's writings on liberty which has dominated our view of the Essay since its publication in 1859 there are a number of common elements. Taken together, they amount to a formidable indictment of Mill's enterprise in *On Liberty*. They suggest that Mill's moral intuitions were at variance with

1

the implications of his moral theory, and that only by seriously com-
promising the one or the other could he have brought the two into
balance. They suggest that the arguments and values he invokes in *On
Liberty* are hopelessly at odds with the utilitarian ethics he espouses
there and elsewhere in his writings, so that *On Liberty*, like Mill himself, could not help being divided against itself. This tradition of criticism and interpretation expresses a conventional view of the intellectual
history of England in the nineteenth century, in which John Stuart Mill
is seen as breaking out of the system of thought of which Bentham and
his father were important exponents, but as never fully admitting to
himself the extent of his apostasy. His thought is naturally perceived,
then, as an eclectic mixture of ill-assorted elements, which tends to fall
apart under any sustained critical pressure. It is irresistibly suggested by
this view of Mill as an eclectic and transitional thinker that his moral
and political writings cannot be expected to yield a coherent doctrine
and that the argument of *On Liberty*, in particular, must inevitably
prove abortive.

It would be a naive error to suppose that Mill's critics of the last
hundred years and more have been in agreement on every important
point in the interpretation of *On Liberty*. Yet common elements in
their interpretations are easily discerned and they frame a criticism of
the book cogent enough and influential enough to be called the
received view of it. Within this received view, we may distinguish three
distinct grounds for the belief that Mill's enterprise in *On Liberty* was
foredoomed to an ignominious failure. The first of these arguments
appeals to the logic of utilitarianism as a single-principle morality. It is
commonly assumed, after all, that a utilitarian will approach every
practical situation with the question: which of all the actions I can perform will bring about the best consequences? Mill says as much himself:
'The creed which accepts as the foundation of morals, Utility, or the
Greatest Happiness Principle, holds that actions are right in proportion
as they tend to promote happiness, wrong as they tend to produce the
reverse of happiness.'⁴ One whose sole goal is the bringing about of best
consequences will not on this account wish to tie his hands as to the
most efficacious strategies for attaining his end. For this reason he will
never adopt as a guide for conduct any maxim which blocks off in
advance some among the alternatives open to him. Most especially, he
will not adopt any maxim which would compel him to discount in his
deliberations any set of good consequences. But this is precisely what
Mill seems to do in *On Liberty*. According to his own avowal in that

book, Mill is committed to viewing the Principle of Utility as framing the terms in which every moral question is to be answered: why then does Mill need another principle when he comes to consider moral questions about limiting liberty? Can he (for that matter) afford another principle? If Mill is truly and consistently a utilitarian moralist, surely every question about the justification of limiting liberty must be answered simply in terms of the good and bad consequences of the various liberty-limiting policies under consideration. A utilitarian moralist can have no use for a principle other than the Principle of Utility itself in any context in which he must decide what to do.

It might be objected against the argument so far that it grossly caricatures utilitarian ethics. After all, a defender of Mill might urge, any sensible utilitarian will acknowledge (as all the great utilitarian writers do) that precepts and maxims more specific than the Principle of Utility itself are useful and even indispensable in the conduct of our practical life. Reasons of economy, limited information and partial sympathies militate strongly against a policy of deciding every practical question by an appeal to the Principle of Utility. So a utilitarian moralist will have a use for principles other than the Principle of Utility, both in contexts of moral instruction and advice and in the ordinary course of his own life. Against this objection, the traditional interpreters of *On Liberty* respond that, however sensible such a procedure might be, it is certainly not adopted by Mill in that essay. In *On Liberty*, they assert, Mill represents his Principle of Liberty, not as a fallible rule-of-thumb, but as an absolute bar against many utility-promoting policies. What does the Principle of Liberty tell us? That no limitation of liberty can ever be sanctioned unless it prevents harm to others. If limiting liberty merely promotes happiness or welfare, say by conferring enormous benefits on many men, it cannot be justified. Mill states his Principle of Liberty as the principle that 'the sole end for which mankind are warranted, individually or collectively, in interfering with the liberty of action of any of their number, is self-protection. That the only purpose for which power can be rightfully exercised over any member of a civilised community, against his will, is to prevent harm to others.'[5] In specifying as a necessary condition of any justified limit on liberty that it prevent harm to others, Mill's Principle of Liberty lays down a necessary and sufficient condition of there being any reason at all for limiting liberty. Now Mill's difficulty is clear and hopeless. According to him, the Principle of Utility must itself supply all reasons for and against any action or policy. Yet we find him in

3

On Liberty urging the adoption of a maxim which is not only distinct in its content from the Principle of Utility, but which actually requires us to disregard the utilitarian effects of actions (and omissions) over an enormously large field. It may be conceded that Mill might have a use for a maxim distinct in content from the Principle of Utility, but it is highly paradoxical to suppose that he might have a use for a maxim which stipulates that the fact that an act promotes utility is no reason at all in favour of doing it, unless it also happens to prevent harm to others.

According to this first strand of objection, then, Mill's difficulty in *On Liberty* results from his attempt to give there a defence in utilitarian terms of a maxim that is not merely different from the Principle of Utility, but which would require anyone who adopted it to ignore the implications of that Principle in a wide range of circumstances. Mill's dilemma here, it has been argued by more recent critics, is only a particularly clear instance of a dilemma that bedevils all utilitarian moralists. Like many others in his tradition, Mill recognises that we cannot always be calculating consequences; we need in our everyday life precepts or rules more specific in their content than the Principle of Utility itself. But, if we are not to renege on our utilitarian commitment, we need always to justify the adoption of these more specific maxims in utilitarian terms. This is to say that these maxims must not be merely consistent with the demands of utility but also derivable from it: they can have no weight beyond that which they possess in virtue of their contribution to utility. They can be only summary rules, rules of thumb which abridge large tracts of complex experience. If they are more than rules of thumb, a utilitarian who treats them as such is abandoning his utilitarian commitment and must be convicted of the error of rule-worship. It is clear from the absolutist language in which the Principle of Liberty is framed that Mill is guilty of just this error of rule-worship in respect of his own principle. He tells us: 'The only part of the conduct of any one, for which he is amendable to society, is that which concerns others. In the part which merely concerns himself, his independence is, of right, absolute. Over himself, over his own body and mind, the individual is sovereign.'[6] Thus Mill constantly treats the Principle of Liberty as if it were not just distinct but somehow independent of the Principle of Utility, as if it were more than just an application of the sovereign utility principle itself. The liberty principle must be other than an application of the Principle of Utility, for that matter, if it is to have any special tenderness for liberty. Mill's problem is

4

precisely in the fact that his Principle of Liberty can be no more than the Principle of Utility at a further remove for as long as he holds to the latter as his ultimate principle.

Whereas this first line of criticism fastens on the logic of utilitarianism as a single-principle morality, a second strand of objection points to the fact that the Principles of Utility and of Liberty protect distinct and often divergent values. While the Principle of Liberty tells us that we may not compromise liberty save where harm to others is at stake, the Principle of Utility tells us that only happiness or pleasure has value for its own sake. Mill's difficulties at once worsen. What reason could there be for thinking of the values of liberty and happiness as being always complementary and mutually supportive, when naturally we think of them as rivals or competitors with one another in many of the dilemmas of civilised life? True, no formal inconsistency is involved in assenting to two exceptionless principles such as 'Always act so as to maximise happiness' and 'In the absence of harm to others, never re- strict liberty'. Mill's problem is that of showing how assent to one exceptionless principle (his Principle of Liberty) is dictated by adher- ence to another such principle (the Principle of Utility). But an excep- tionless principle about the conditions under which liberty may rightly be limited will have the same implications for practice as the principle of utility only on very questionable assumptions about the predicta- bility and regularity of human affairs. On any realistically plausible view of man and society, serious losses of happiness must sometimes result from uncompromising adherence to such a principle. An exact coincidence of the implications of the two principles must be judged to be marvellously unlikely. Given that his principles encapsulate distinct and sometimes conflicting values, what reason could Mill give for re- fusing to allow his supreme principle to override the liberty principle whenever the two conflict? So long as he remains a utilitarian, surely, nothing can be allowed to override the application of the utility principle; but the force of his liberty principle is precisely to debar appeal to utility in defence of limiting liberty except in a very restricted range of circumstances. If liberty and utility are indeed distinct values, must they not sometimes be in competition with each other? And, in such circumstances of competition, how could a utilitarian consistently accord priority to liberty?

At this point, it might be urged in defence of Mill that he did not suppose utility or happiness to be as distinct from liberty as the criti- cisms we have been expounding suppose it to be. He tells us that the utility of which he speaks 'must be utility in the largest sense, grounded on the permanent interests of man as a progressive being'.[7] The point of immediately qualifying his endorsement of utilitarian ethics with a reference to 'utility in the largest sense' in the opening pages of *On Liberty* might reasonably be to indicate that Mill takes happiness to include, perhaps as necessary ingredients, elements such as individuality and self-development. These elements of happiness might themselves, in turn, be partly constituted by conditions having to do with (or containing) liberty.

Now it may easily be conceded against this objection that to speak of liberty and happiness as if they were entirely distinct values would run against the tenor of Mill's writings. Even if this concession is made, his difficulty remains. Liberty and happiness cannot plausibly be identified with each other; happiness has among its conditions and ingredients many things other than liberty of which a utilitarian theorist is bound to take note. Again, even if liberty is ranked as one among the necessary ingredients of happiness, it seems unwarranted to accord it an infinite weight in any conflict with the other necessary ingredients. Nor are instances hard to find where other ingredients necessary to happiness compete with liberty. The happiness of many men is bound up with the attainment of illiberal ideals, by which their preferences are informed and shaped, and policies guided mainly by concern for the promotion of happiness (or the satisfaction of preferences) will not normally conform to liberal principles. Indeed, if liberalism is itself defined as a doctrine dictating that preferences be maximally satisfied, regardless of any ideals other than those expressed in men's actual preferences (as Barry, who conceives of liberalism in this fashion, has perceived[8]), then it will have a self-defeating effect. For, on any ordinary estimate, liberty is not always or even generally the weightiest element in human happiness. To accord to liberty, conceived as a necessary ingredient of happiness, such a weight that it can never rightly be compromised for the sake of any of the other ingredients is merely to resort to stipulation without good reason and to retreat from serious consideration of practical dilemmas of just the sort to which *On Liberty* is supposedly addressed.

Any utilitarian argument for liberty in which it is stipulated that happiness cannot be in competition with liberty has a question-begging aspect. Now it might be thought that Mill's argument is not that happiness can never come into conflict with other values; rather, it is that happiness must be conceived of in a specific fashion, so that it embodies or desiderates a definite conception of personal excellence. Apart from the point that it is not clear how such a restrictive view of happiness could be argued for or made plausible, such a move compromises one of the chief features often held to be characteristic of liberalism,[9] and an aspect of liberalism on which Mill himself often dwells. This is that the institutions of a liberal society, and thus the basic principles of liberalism which these institutions exemplify, are neutral with respect to rival views of personal excellence. A liberal may indeed be wedded to a specific conception of the good life, and he may well think a liberal society most congenial to its promotion and achievement; but he will not think of the principles and institutions of liberal society as promoting his own conception of the good life at the expense of other competing views. A utilitarian argument for liberty, in which some ideals of life are excluded from consideration as aspects of well-being, might be judged to be one in which something of the spirit of liberalism has been lost, even if it fails to support the view of Mill as a moral totalitarian[10], or to involve him in any sort of logical inconsistency.

It is the burden of the second strand of criticism we have explored that Mill's Principles of Liberty and of Utility invoke or desiderate distinct values which may conflict with one another. Where they do conflict, Mill must in consistency with his overriding utilitarian commitment give priority to happiness over liberty. Because these two values conflict in practice, there is not even a constant conjunction of them: any generalisation according to which liberty goes with happiness must be uncomfortably exception-ridden. This is of some importance for Mill's enterprise inasmuch as any utilitarian argument is in principle reversible and if, as his critics suggest, liberty is not always the most efficient means to happiness, Mill is bound then to endorse illiberal policies instead. In the third line of criticism which is found in Mill's traditional critics, the first two strands are drawn together and some new elements added. It has already been maintained that no utility-barring maxim such as the Principle of Liberty could possibly have a utilitarian derivation. The third and, for many of his critics, crucial objection to Mill's enterprise is that the principle of Liberty he seeks to defend in utilitarian terms is a utility-barring principle of a specific kind, namely, one that assigns weighty moral claims to individuals. It is, in short, a principle which distributes moral rights. But no such rights-conferring principle can be given a satisfactory utilitarian derivation or defence. Any principle of utility at all recognisable as such must be aggregative in form, that is to say, it must have as its subject matter

7

the sum of happiness in existence or to be produced by action. The Principle of Liberty, on the other hand, is pre-eminently distributive in character: it attaches rights to their bearers and says nothing about maximising or even promoting any value. Mill's liberty principle seems naturally an element in a theory of justice rather than of the good. A theory of what is good may, no doubt, be necessary to specify the content of the rights distributed under a conception of justice, but the point still remains that the Principle of Liberty is indifferent to the aggregate amount of good that its implementation might yield. The point could be put more strongly inasmuch as Mill's Principle of Liberty is most naturally seen as a principle imposing a moral constraint on the pursuit of happiness rather than as capturing an efficient strategy for its promotion.

It ought to be reasonably clear how this third objection trades upon and develops the sense of the other two. It had already been argued that Mill's utilitarian morality has room for only one moral principle — the Principle of Utility itself. Mill can accordingly find no place for principles of obligation or of right in his picture of the moral life. For a utilitarian, it is supposed, obligation and rightness must be indistinguishable: the only duty anyone can ever have is to bring about the best consequences. As G.E. Moore, himself an adherent of this view, puts it, 'it must always be the duty of every agent to do that one, among all actions which he can do on any given occasion, whose *total consequences* will have the greatest intrinsic value'.[11] It was further suggested that the two principles invoke distinct and conflicting values. It is now urged that they are, in effect, principles of a radically different kind. For some critics, indeed, that the Principle of Liberty cannot be derived from utility follows inexorably from its character as a principle conferring moral rights of some sort on individuals. Dworkin, for example, sees rights as essentially invoking moral constraints on the pursuit of general welfare,[12] whereas Nozick[13] conceives of his side-constraints or moral rights as framing boundaries against maximisation or minimisation of any sort of value. Other recent writers, such as Lucas,[14] agree in so far as they see the subject-matter of rights as inherently distributive.

Mill's seems to have the worst of both worlds. On the one hand, in laying down that no amount of benefit but only the prevention of harm to others can justify restricting liberty, Mill's principle imposes a moral constraint on the pursuit of utility that is indefensible in utilitarian terms. On the other hand, in allowing that utilitarian considerations re-emerge as paramount once the barrier presented to them by the Principle of Liberty has been crossed, he still does not succeed in avoiding the old conflicts of justice with general welfare. A minor but very widespread kind of harm might be prevented cost-effectively but very inequitably by policies which, though they passed the test of the Principle of Liberty, heaped great burdens on a small section of the community. There seems then no obstacle in principle within utilitarian morality to a policy which indeed prevents harm but at the expense of the most basic interests of a minority. So it may be that, even if the Principle of Liberty were derivable from Utility, Mill would need another principle to stave off such possibilities. Such a principle could only be an independent principle of equity or fairness. It remains unclear how such a principle could be given a utilitarian derivation since (as Mill himself elsewhere explicitly states[15]) individuals figure as equals in utilitarian morality, not as bearers of equal rights, but only as placeholders for pleasures whose value is to be calculated without regard to the identity of the person to whom they are attributed. It is the burden of this third line of criticism that the two principles with which Mill works in *On Liberty* cannot be related in the ways he suggests, if only because they invoke considerations (distributive and aggregative) of radically different kinds. Here it is argued that no utilitarian defence of a distributive principle could ever succeed inasmuch as it would have to achieve the impossible task of deriving one sort of principle from another which is irreducibly different. In so far as this third criticism encapsulates and builds upon the previous two, it has widely been thought to clinch the argument that in *On Liberty* Mill is seeking to square the circle.

2 A REVISIONARY VIEW

In the current of destructive criticism which has dominated Mill scholarship during much of the century since the publication of *On Liberty* a number of common elements may be discerned, and I have marked three of these in the exposition I have given of the main grounds Mill's critics have adduced for their view that his enterprise in *On Liberty* is radically misconceived. If anyone wants an example of what I have called the traditional criticism of Mill on liberty, he can do no better than turn to James Fitzjames Stephen's *Liberty, Equality, Fraternity*[16] in which all three elements are strikingly evident. In this, still by far the most powerful criticism of Mill's doctrine of liberty, Stephen maintains that Mill has no need and can have no use for a principle specially designed to protect liberty in that, for Mill, utility itself must be the sole test of the justification of all policies and institutions. Further, Stephen argues, liberty and happiness are wholly distinct, and liberty can have no intrinsic value within a utilitarian morality, still less can it have any priority when it competes with the demands of utility. Finally, Stephen insists, talk of moral rights has always been and ought in consistency to remain foreign to the utilitarian outlook on political questions. Stephen's argument illustrates in particularly clear form a number of assumptions, taken for granted by most of Mill's critics, which have been put in question by a new wave of Mill scholarship which emerged in the 1960s. It is the upshot of this wave of revisionary interpretation[17] that traditional criticisms of Mill's writings on liberty and utility display an insensitivity to the subtlety and complexity of the argument of *On Liberty* and neglect the many connections holding between the argument of that book and the doctrines set out in several of his other writings. We may say even more forcefully of *On Liberty* what one of Mill's revisionary interpreters[18] has recently said of *Utilitarianism*:

> The traditional interpretation of Mill is certainly mistaken; indeed, given its currency, it is surprising just how little textual support there is for it. It is not a construal to which an impartial reader can be led by a careful study of *Utilitarianism*, and its persistence is largely due to the enormous influence of Moore.

In general, we can now see that much of the traditional account of Mill's utilitarianism is simply wrong. More specifically, it is common ground among Mill's new interpreters that the argument of *On Liberty* (1859) cannot properly be understood or criticised unless it is set in the context of the theory of the Art of Life which is elaborated in the *System of Logic* (1843) and linked with the account of justice and moral rights developed in the last chapter of *Utilitarianism* (composed between 1854 and 1859, published in *Fraser's Magazine* for October-December 1861).

Just as there are important differences among Mill's traditional critics which it would be wrong to neglect, so it would be a mistake to suppose that Mill's new interpreters are in agreement on every important question in the exegesis of Mill's moral and political writings. There is a large area of common ground, however, in which the new interpretation of Mill draws attention to a range of neglected connections between Mill's writings and focuses on a set of distinctions at work in several of the most important of his books — distinctions which have gone almost wholly ignored until recent decades. It will be one of my tasks later in this book to set out clearly and to try to settle some of the disputes among Mill's newer interpreters. At this stage, it is worth laying down in greater detail the outlines of that area of common ground occupied by all of them. Thus it is now acknowledged that much of the argument of *On Liberty* turns on a set of distinctions, adumbrated there and elsewhere in the body of Mill's writings, between questions of justice, obligation and right conduct, on the one hand, and of value, on the other. Making sense of Mill's doctrine of liberty presupposes an understanding of the account of the Art of Life set out in *A System of Logic*, in which the Principle of Utility figures, not as a moral principle from which may be derived in any very direct way judgments about the rightness of actions, but as an axiological principle specifying that happiness alone has intrinsic goodness. Though the Principle of Utility has no direct bearing on action or conduct, it gives reasons for and against any course of action or policy in all areas of practical life, but cannot itself yield judgments about the rightness or wrongness of actions. The Principle of Liberty, on the other hand, is a principle of critical morality, which has important (though often misunderstood) implications for the rightness and justice of acts and rules. These two principles are of such different logical types that the relations between them cannot perspicuously be characterised in terms of extensional equivalence or non-equivalence — in terms, that is to say, of their implications when they are applied in practice. What, then, according to Mill's account of the Art of Life, is the relation between the Principle of Utility and moral principles such as his Principle of Liberty?

Determining in fine detail the exact character of this relation, by far the most controversial point in the new interpretation of Mill's Doctrine of Liberty, will occupy me at length in the next chapter of this book. In broad outline, though, it is common ground among Mill's new interpreters that the Principle of Utility figures in Mill's moral and political thought, not as a principle of right action, but as a general principle of valuation. In Mill's conception of it, the Principle of Utility is an axiological principle specifying that happiness and that alone has intrinsic goodness. As an axiological principle — a principle specifying what is of value for its own sake — the Principle of Utility has no direct bearing on action at all. Only with the assistance of other principles such as Mill's Principle of Expediency (on which I shall have more to say later) can the bearing on action of the Principle of Utility be assessed. The Principle of Expediency, which Mill never states explicitly but for which there is ample evidence in his writings, is a consequentialist principle specifying that that act is maximally expedient and ought to be done which has the best consequences. Taken together, Mill's Principle of Utility and the Principle of Expediency yield as a theorem the principle that that act ought to be done which produces the most happiness. We come now to a turning-point in the new interpretation of Mill on liberty and utility. If, as I have suggested, Mill holds to both his Principle of Utility and a consequentialist principle, what use can he have for any other principle such as the Principle of Liberty? On this question, and on the general question of the relation between utility as an axiological principle and other, action-guiding principles in Mill, there is no consensus among Mill's recent interpreters. Some hold on textual and logical grounds that Mill's moral theory has room for principles such as his Principle of Liberty only if Mill is committed to some form of rule-utilitarianism, while others maintain that such principles may be accommodated within Mill's doctrine if we ascribe to him a sophisticated version of act-utilitarianism. I shall argue myself for the view that Mill's position cannot be captured in any modern distinction between 'act' and 'rule' variants of utilitarianism. Mill is best interpreted as holding to a version of *indirect utilitarianism* wherein the Principle of Utility cannot have direct application either to individual acts or to social rules because such application is in general, and in many cases necessarily, self-defeating. One of my aims in this book is not merely to show that this was the form of Mill's utilitarianism, but also to suggest that it comprehends a theory of practical reasoning and of morality which is interesting and (with important qualifications) plausible.

On any interpretation of Mill on liberty in which his theory of the Art of Life is seen as crucially relevant, it will be acknowledged that many of the elements of the traditional critique of his doctrine miss the mark. For, first, whatever its exact bearings on action, the Principle of Utility in Mill is not a moral principle of the same kind as his Principle of Liberty, and no straightforward conflict or competition between them is possible. As an axiological principle, the Principle of Utility cannot itself yield judgments about what ought to be done, so it is utterly mistaken to argue (as do those who hold to the first strand of of criticism of Mill) that he can have no need for any principles, precepts or maxims other than the Principle of Utility. Any utilitarian, even an act-utilitarian, can in any case have a use for maxims distinct from the Principle of Utility for the reasons I have sketched above. If Mill's indirect utilitarianism be accepted and the direct application of the Principle of Utility is acknowledged to be self-defeating, then a utilitarian may have reason to act on a secondary maxim, even in the paradoxical circumstance where doing so appears to result in a loss of achievable happiness. If Mill's indirect utilitarianism is at all credible, then secondary maxims – precepts distinct from utility and having implications other than those resulting from a straightforward calcula- tion of consequences – are not just helpful but actually indispensable to the utilitarian's practical life. It is just such secondary principles, practical precepts for the guidance of conduct, that Mill seeks to supply in his doctrine of the Art of Life as set out in the *Logic*. For here Mill proposes that the whole of practical life be carved up into a number of departments or branches – Morality, Prudence and Excellence (which he sometimes calls Aesthetics or Nobility) being the classification he adopts most consistently – where various maxims are to govern conduct in these three areas. Second, because the principles of Utility and of Liberty are in Mill principles of such different types, they cannot compete in the simple way suggested by those who see them as invoking divergent values. Further, as I will myself argue in chapter 3, Mill has in his view of human nature and his theory of individuality sound reasons for resisting too drastic a disseveration of liberty from happiness. Third, the key element in all recent interpretations of Mill is that utility in Mill, though it frames the terms in which his theory of morality must be understood and defended, is not itself a moral principle of either an aggregative or a distributive sort. This is the feature of Mill's doctrine which is neglected by those who, arguing that distributive and aggregative considerations are incommensurables, hold that a utilitarian theory of justice and of moral rights is a conceptual impossibility. All variants of the revisionary interpretation suggest that there is nothing incoherent or inadvertent in Mill's project of building up a theory of justice in which the moral right to liberty has priority. It may yet be shown that his theory fails, but, if so, it does not fail because it is from the start misconceived. The theory of the Art of Life opens up the possibility that, in respecting other's rights in circumstan- ces where this involves a loss of utility, men may not be acting wrongly, even though they act inexpediently. For it is just the point of the theory of the Art of Life to distinguish between different sorts of judgment about what ought to be done — judgments of expediency, of morality, of obligation and of justice. Though there is space in Mill's diverse statements on these matters for reasonable difference of opinion, there can be no doubt that he does work with these distinctions and that they do enable him to resist some of the most familiar criticisms of his doctrine.

3 THE ARGUMENT OF THIS BOOK

In part my task in this book will be to elucidate the new pattern of interpretation of Mill's writings on liberty and utility that has emerged in the last fifteen years, to settle some important differences among the new interpretations and to resolve some difficulties in the revisionary work that has been done so far on Mill. More ambitiously, however, I wish to show that Mill's writings contain a coherent and forceful utilitarian defence of liberal principles about the right to liberty. We arrive at a clear view of Mill's utilitarian theory of the right to liberty only by seeing the argument of *On Liberty* in the terms of the account of justice and moral rights in *Utilitarianism* and of the nature of the Principle of Utility as it is explained in the relevant chapters of *A System of Logic*. The essays on *Utilitarianism* and *On Liberty* were written around the same time (1854-9) and, though they were addressed to an audience of intelligent laymen rather than to one of philosophers, they take for granted much that is argued about the Art of Life in *A System of Logic* (1843) where Mill had other philosophers as his intended audience. My submission will be that, once these writings of Mill's have been put together and their various contributions integrated, we find in Mill a powerful defence of liberal principles which has three important features. First, Mill's doctrine of liberty rests on a form of indirect utilitarianism in which there is room for weighty secondary principles, including moral principles to do with justice and moral rights. Second, Mill's doctrine of liberty draws upon his conception of happiness and on his theory of individuality; it is almost unintelligible when wrenched out of that context. His defence of liberty is, indeed, so deeply embedded in his conception of man and in his account of the development of character that some of his critics have suspected that the relations he argues for between liberty, self-development and happiness are no more than a series of analytical equivalences. This is a view (depending on a view of necessity as analyticity or equivalence in meaning which Mill could not have endorsed) which I shall show to be mistaken. It is true that Mill's conception of human nature does not stand in relation to his defence of the value of liberty as might an ordinary body of facts. Mill's account of man aims to identify features of human life which, though they might conceivably have been otherwise and so are in that respect contingent, at the same time are so much beyond our powers of alteration as to be presupposed by all sensible reflection on the conditions of our moral and political life. There is in Mill's account of the conditions of a stable social order and in his implicit account of the criteria for harm to others a view of the unalterable requirements of social life akin to that which Hart has advanced in his theses about the minimum content of natural law.[19] But, third, in that it rests on a number of psychological and historical claims about the social conditions of individuality and self-development, Mill's doctrine of liberty is open to criticism by an appeal to experience even though it cannot easily be overturned by a change in the facts. Mill's doctrine of liberty postulates connections between liberty, self-development and happiness which are neither simply causal nor merely conceptual. If his doctrine is at all successful, it should show us how a utilitarian theory may be based on contingent facts about human life and yet not stand in constant need of revision as society changes just in virtue of that contingent basis.

In my interpretation of it, the structure of Mill's utilitarian argument for the moral right to liberty is such that it depends on three claims. First, there is a claim about the self-defeating effect of direct appeals to utility: it is in virtue of certain contingent (but none the less unalterable) features of man and society, mainly to do with the distinctive features of human happiness and with the conditions necessary to social co-operation, that Mill recommends the adoption of a principle constraining the direct pursuit of happiness as a self-denying ordinance with respect to the promotion of happiness.[20] This is a relatively formal thesis, inasmuch as it maintains that a principle constraining the pursuit of happiness is derivable from principles which enjoin maximising it with the assistance of certain quasi-empirical assumptions about the paradoxical and self-defeating effects of trying directly to promote happiness, but it says nothing as yet of the content of the principle so derived. If this principle assigns moral rights to men, for example, we do not yet know which rights — rights to welfare, say, or to non-interference — and we do not know how these rights are to be weighted in cases where they conflict with each other. There is, second, accordingly, a historical claim in developmental human psychology: with the unfolding of powers of autonomous thought and action, Mill contends, men come to derive satisfaction increasingly from activities involving the exercise of these powers. For such men, happiness or pleasure is not any passive state of contentment, but is found only in activity – in activity, moreover, in which indefinitely many diverse projects are undertaken and subjected to recurrent revision and criticism. In this second claim, Mill's Aristotelian conception of happiness is linked with his Humboldtian view of individuality. Third, there is the claim that it is in a liberal social order that the powers of men, having once reached the level necessary to take them out of barbarism, are further refined and developed, and indefinitely many forms of happiness involving the exercise of these powers discovered and elaborated upon. These are all more or less empirical claims, revisable by experience, but, if they are once granted, there can be nothing inadvertent or incoherent in Mill's utilitarian argument for moral rights or for the priority he assigns to the right to liberty.

Once the coherence of Mill's version of indirect utilitarianism has been allowed, it becomes possible to see how a utilitarian morality may contain weighty rights-conferring principles. The self-defeating effect of acting according to a direct calculation of best consequences suggests the necessity (for a utilitarian) of practical maxims which bar such action (at least in certain circumstances, which I will try to specify later). Mill argues for the adoption of his Principle of Liberty, in effect, in virtue of its being that utility-barring maxim whose observance will have the best utility-promoting effects. The liberty of action that is protected by the Principle of Liberty is protected as a moral right, whose content is given in part by the theory of justice of which it is an element, and in part by referring to a restrictive conception of harm which Mill argues for by invoking a theory of men's vital interests in autonomy and security. This moral right is a defeasible right (like the moral rights established in many non-utilitarian theories of justice) but it is not to be overridden whenever a calculation of consequences seems to suggest this might yield a net utility benefit, it grounds obligations not derivable directly from the demands of utility and it is not conferred simply because of the benefits it will yield in any particular case. In order to see how to apply the Principle of Liberty, and to see if its application by Mill is consistently utilitarian, we need to look at his doctrine as a whole. This doctrine will be found to contain principles other than the Principle of Liberty – for example, a Principle of Equity, never named or stated explicitly by Mill, but often mentioned by him in *On Liberty* as laying down how much liberty may be given up for how much harm-prevention. The utilitarian character of Mill's Doctrine of Liberty as a whole will be preserved if these other principles, along with the Principle of Liberty itself, can be shown to have a utilitarian derivation and justification, and if the theory of the Art of Life (of which Mill's theory of justice and his Doctrine of Liberty are only a part) can itself be defended in utilitarian terms.

In the course of my argument, I will cover a number of well-trodden areas of Mill scholarship and criticism. In general, the result of my exploration will be that Mill rarely commits the crude fallacies often attributed to him. His account of moral knowledge involves him in no important naturalistic fallacy, and his famous 'proof' of utility does not commit a fallacy of composition. Mill's philosophical psychology is more sophisticated than most intellectual historians or critics have allowed, and it is mistaken to ascribe to Mill any doctrine of psychological egoism. The much-abused distinction between higher and lower pleasures will be seen as a distinction between forms of life and activity which, when it is framed in the context of the theory of individuality outlined in *On Liberty*, preserves the want-regarding character of the Principle of Utility. In none of these familiar areas does Mill commit the howlers that it is common to ascribe to him.

My main object will not be to clear Mill of all the charges of fallacy or obscurity which have been levelled against various aspects of his moral and general philosophy, but to identify and defend the chief tenets of what I shall call his Doctrine of Liberty. Mill's Doctrine of Liberty, as I shall define it, is independent of many of the claims of his general philosophy and might be endorsed even by one who could not accept the broader commitments of Mill's liberalism. The Doctrine of Liberty includes the various principles stated and defended in *On Liberty*, together with the pattern of argument developed in that essay and elsewhere in Mill's writings in their support. It is an important task in interpreting Mill to ascertain just what are the principles defended in *On Liberty* and which are the arguments in their support that Mill himself considered crucial. Identifying the component arguments and principles of the Doctrine of Liberty allows us to see that that doctrine is silent about the proper limits of state activity and contains no commitment to any principle of *laissez-faire*. Mill's Doctrine of Liberty is a narrower one than the doctrines encompassed by liberalism, classical or contemporary. It is compatible with some variants of socialism and social democracy and no less compatible with some doctrines of the minimum functions of the state. Its defence is to be conducted apart from that of the broader commitments of liberalism, whether it be Mill's liberalism or our own.

At the level of criticism, it will be my aim to defend the Doctrine of Liberty, and to argue that, though it does not achieve all that Mill on occasion demanded of it, it is not an absurd or incoherent doctrine, or one that is vulnerable to those traditional criticisms generally held to be most telling. I will admit that, though it cannot reasonably be claimed that experience tells decisively against the psychological and historical claims which support the Doctrine of Liberty, still the Doctrine lacks that solid basis in a science of human nature that Mill hoped for it. For us, as indeed for Mill, the commitment to liberty cannot avoid having the aspect of a wager since we are little better placed than was Mill to put our commonsensical knowledge of human life on a scientific footing. Again, I will admit that, even when taken in the context of the entire Doctrine of Liberty, the Principle of Liberty defended by Mill does not supply an unequivocal yardstick for the resolution of questions of interference with liberty. A major failing of Mill's argument is its neglect of problems of conflict of values in moral and political life and of the limited role that appeals to principle or theory can have in resolving such dilemmas. At the same time, even though it cannot mechanically resolve all questions to do with interference with liberty, Mill's doctrine does supply a framework of considerations in terms of which such questions may be discussed. More incisively, it rules out from the discussion a whole range of considerations still widely invoked as germane to it. And it supports this exclusion by making claims about the place of liberty in our lives that are reasonable and plausible even though they have yet to be grounded in a science of human nature. The Doctrine of Liberty developed by Mill and defended in this book remains today as arguable and as controversial as it was when *On Liberty* was published.

II

MILL'S UTILITARIANISM

1 THE ART OF LIFE AND UTILITY AS AN AXIOLOGICAL PRINCIPLE

The point of departure of Mill's theory of the Art of Life is his distinction between scientific laws and practical injunctions. In *A System of Logic* Mill spoke of the Logic of Practice or Art as being expressed in the imperative mood, whereas that of science is expressed in indicatives. The Logic of Practice has as its subject matter the ends of action, or teleology, and seeks to classify these ends into departments or families and settle conflicts between them. Several points need clarification and emphasis in this brief characterisation. First, whereas Mill insists forcefully on the importance of the distinction between art and science, he is nevertheless at pains to stress that practical precepts are grounded in or supported by the theorems of the appropriate science. Precepts of practice or art cannot be justified by any theorem of science, but they always presuppose some such theorems. Each practical art — architecture and medicine are examples Mill gives[1] — 'has one first principle, or major premise, not borrowed from science; that which enuciates the object aimed at, and affirms it to be a desirable object'.[2] Mill goes on to assert that the various principles or premises of the practical arts[3]

together with the principal conclusions which may be deduced from them, form (or rather might form) a body of doctrine, which is properly the Art of Life, in its three departments, Morality, Prudence or Policy, and Aesthetics; the Right, the Expedient, and the Beautiful or Noble, in human conduct and works. To this art

19

(which, in the main, is unfortunately still to be created) all other arts are subordinate; since its principles are those which must determine whether the special aim of any particular art is worthy or desirable, and what is its place in the scale of desirable things. Every art is thus a joint result of the laws of nature disclosed by science, and of the general principles of what has been called Teleology, or the Doctrine of Ends; which . . . may also be termed, the Principles of Practical Reasoning.

Against the intuitionist doctrine that right action is somehow directly evident to us in each case, Mill is concerned to show that a first principle is needed to settle conflicts among the precepts of the various departments or branches of the Art of Life. This one first principle gives us the Philosophia Prima peculiar to Art or Practice and is none other than the Principle of Utility: for, as Mill puts it in the *Logic*, 'the promotion of happiness is the ultimate principle of Teleology'. How does utility inform the Art of Life and yield practical precepts in morality and elsewhere?

Any account of Mill's understanding of the character and uses of the Principle of Utility must begin by admitting that Mill gives us many statements of it. D.G. Brown refers to 'fifteen possible formulations (of the Principle of Utility) which Mill seems committed to regarding as equivalent' and confesses that the version of the principle he at length identifies as closest to Mill's intention is not without its difficulties.[4] It is a common feature of the most central of Mill's formulations of the principle, however, that Utility figures as a principle of appraisal of all aspects of life and as the test of all conduct. Thus, in the second chapter of the essay on *Utilitarianism*, Mill defines utilitarianism as follows:[5]

The creed which accepts as the foundation of morals, Utility, or the Greatest Happiness Principle, holds that actions are right in proportion as they tend to promote happiness, wrong as they tend to produce the reverse of happiness. By happiness is intended pleasure and the absence of pain; by unhappiness, pain, and the privation of pleasure. To give a clear view of the moral standard set up by the theory much more requires to be said: in particular, what things it includes in the ideas of pain and pleasure; and to what extent this is left an open question. But these supplementary questions do not affect the theory of life on which this theory of morality is grounded — namely, that pleasure, and freedom from pain, are the only things desirable as ends; and that all desirable things (which are as numerous in the utilitarian as in any other scheme) are desirable either for the pleasure inherent in themselves, or as means to the promotion of pleasure and the prevention of pain.

This is not an altogether perspicuous passage. It begins by connecting the Principle of Utility in a general sort of way with the rightness and wrongness of actions. It goes on, however, to distinguish 'the moral standard set up by the theory' from 'the theory of life on which this theory of morality is grounded'. According to this 'theory of life', only pleasure and the absence of pain are desirable as ends. Later in the same chapter, Mill tells us that:[6]

According to the Greatest Happiness Principle, as above explained, the ultimate end, with reference to and for the sake of which all other things are desirable (whether we are considering our own good or that of other people) is an existence exempt as far as possible from pain, and as rich as possible in enjoyments . . . This being, according to utilitarian opinion, the end of human action, is necessarily also the standard of morality; which may accordingly be defined, the rules and precepts for human conduct, by the observance of which an existence such as has been described might be, to the greatest extent possible, secured to all mankind.

Again, in the chapter in which a proof of the principle is attempted, Mill says succinctly: 'The utilitarian doctrine is, that happiness is desirable, and the only thing desirable, as an end'.[7] I think it a reasonable inference from these and other, similar formulations, that the Principle of Utility, as Mill conceived of it, specifies that happiness alone is desirable as an end, where by happiness Mill intended pleasure and the absence of pain. In Mill this principle ranges over all areas of practice, not only moral practice, and, indeed, functions as a principle of evaluation for things apart from human practices and actions. Since moral appraisal is only one sort of appraisal of conduct, and morality is only one area of practice or art, the Principle of Utility cannot be treated as if its place in Mill's moral theory is simply that of a moral principle. Since the Principle of Utility in Mill is a principle for the assessment of all branches of conduct, and since it specifies what is of intrinsic value but does not itself enjoin any particular line of conduct, those writers of the traditional school in Mill criticism are in error who suppose that the utility principle must impose a moral duty of utility-maximisation on agents. This is to say that, if the Principle of Utility figures directly at the critical level but not generally at the practical level of moral thought, it cannot by itself impose obligations or yield judgments about right action.

A number of questions need answering, however, before we can be satisfied that we have in this revisionary view an interpretation of Mill's theory of morality which yields a coherent and defensible view. What exactly are the demands made on action by the utility principle as it has here been construed? If the utility principle is indeed categorically different from any practical principle, how could any moral principle — the Principle of Liberty, say — be derived from it or even be supported by it? On these questions Mill's statements are not very clear: as I have already observed, he says within a single paragraph that 'the creed which accepts as the foundation of Morals, Utility, or the Greatest Happiness Principle, holds that actions are right in proportion as they tend to produce happiness, wrong as they tend to produce the reverse of happiness'; and he later clarifies the 'theory of life' on which this 'theory of morality' is grounded as specifying that 'pleasure, and freedom from pain, are the only things desirable as ends'.[8] In these somewhat murky statements Mill seems to be acknowledging the utility principle as primarily axiological in character, while yet insisting that conclusions about action somehow flow from it. The combination of these two claims has spawned an enormous interpretive literature on the question of the structure of Mill's utilitarianism. According to the revisionary account, it should be clear, in the first place, that, whatever it may be, the utility principle cannot in Mill's account of it range solely over actions. As a principle specifying what is of value in the world, it will serve as a standard of assessment of states of affairs, even where there is nothing that can be done to affect them. (It would enable us to judge a state of affairs in which a solitary wild animal dies slowly of a painful disease a bad state of affairs, though it is one that no one's actions have produced or could alter.) The Principle of Utility does not, then, apply solely to action, and, since it applies to other areas of life as well, it cannot be only a moral principle. But is the Principle of Utility in any sense a moral principle and does it apply to action at all? It is common within the revisionary interpretation to distinguish another principle, distinct from the Principle of Utility, which does have action as its subject-matter. This is the principle, often invoked by Mill under the name expediency but nowhere named by him, which (following several of the recent interpreters) I will call the

Principle of Expediency. According to this principle, an act is expedient if it brings about a net utility benefit, and maximally expedient if it brings about as much utility as any available alternative act. Mill invokes this principle in order to distinguish judgments of the morality and rightness of acts from questions of their expediency or utility-promoting effect: according to Mill, when a man acts inexpediently, he does not necessarily act wrongly. How the expediency of an act is related to its rightness is a topic I will address later: but how is expediency connected with utility? Is the Principle of Expediency necessarily implied by the Principle of Utility, or are the two principles quite independent of one another? And how does the answer to this question bear on the structure of Mill's utilitarian ethics?

What follows if the expediency principle issues inexorably from the Principle of Utility? If so, the sharp contrast between utility as an axiological principle and liberty as a practical (action-guiding) principle is blurred. For, whereas the principles of Utility and Expediency might not be equivalent, the expediency principle does seem to embody a maximising approach to whatever has utility. In such a case, endorsement of the utility principle would appear to entail adoption of a maximisation strategy about utility, and the ancient competition between utility and liberty re-emerges as a contest between expediency and liberty. Any principle about the restriction of liberty that is defensible in utilitarian terms must then be an application of the Principle of Utility itself, if the competition between liberty and happiness is to be resolved within the framework of Mill's doctrine. What we have here is none other than the traditional objection to Mill's enterprise in *On Liberty*, powerfully restated by Honderich. Speaking of what he characterises as '*the* Utilitarian principle about intervention', Honderich observes that 'there is little to be said for it. What I mean is that it is no advance on something we have been entertaining throughout these reflections. What we have come to is patently the Principle of Utility as applied to the question of intervention'.[9] For Honderich, then, the Principle of Liberty must either be ultimately indistinguishable from the Principle of Utility or else indefensible in terms of it. What can be said in answer to these difficulties?

Two remarks are in order. First, it is not at all self-evident that the Principles of Utility and of Expediency are as intimately related as I have thus far assumed. They are plainly distinct principles, and it is at least not obvious that anyone who accepts such an axiological principle is thereby committed to maximising whatever the principle tells him has value for its own sake. He might, for example, treat such an axiological principle as framing the boundaries of permissible action, forbidding him from action which tends to diminish the amount of utility already in the world, but not enjoining him to increase it, still less to maximise it. In any case, the notion of intrinsic value is itself so opaque that no one can with complete confidence elicit practical maxims from axiological principles which state only wherein it consists. There seem to be two rival views of the relation between principles which specify what has intrinsic value and principles which have strong action-guiding force. One view is that of Prichard, who draws on Rashdall's discussion of the question and says:[10]

> Consider . . . what may be called Utilitarianism in the generic sense, in which what is good is not limited to pleasure. It takes its stand upon the distinction between something which is not itself an action, but which can be produced by an action, and the action which will produce it, and contends that if something which is not an action is good, then *we ought* to undertake the action which will, directly or indirectly, originate it.
>
> But this argument, if it is to restore the sense of obligation to act, must presuppose an intermediate link, viz., the further thesis that what is good ought to be. The necessity of this link is obvious. An 'ought', if it is to be derived at all, can only be derived from another 'ought'. Moreover, the link tacitly presupposes another, viz., that the apprehension that something good which is not an action ought to be, involves just the feeling of imperativeness or obligation which is to be aroused by the thought of the action which will originate it. Otherwise the argument will not lead us to feel the obligation to produce it by the action.

On Prichard's view, nothing follows for action from the claim that something has intrinsic value, even where it is claimed that one thing and that thing alone has intrinsic value. For some writers in the utilitarian tradition, on the other hand, claims about intrinsic value must entail claims about reasons for action: for what could be meant by asserting that something has intrinsic value other than that (other things being equal) we have reason to bring it about? Those two views of the relation between statements about intrinsic value and statements about action are mirrored in the recent revisionary literature on Mill. Lyons seems ready to concur with a view akin to Prichard's, and affirms that utility as a principle about ultimate ends or intrinsic value makes no claim on action of any sort, rational or moral.[11]

Dryer adopts a different view in his exposition of Mill:[12]

> He argues that it is because happiness is the only thing desirable for its own sake that the test of conduct generally is its promotion of happiness. The principle he employs in taking this step is that, if there is one sort of thing that is desirable for its own sake, then the promotion of it is the test of all human conduct . . . Mill takes it for granted that something should be done if and only if its consequences would be more desirable than would those of any alternative to it.

Dryer's statement of Mill's view seems sound. It suggests that Mill's utilitarianism comprehends two distinct principles, the Principle of Utility proper (conceived of as an axiological principle stipulating that happiness alone has intrinsic value) and the Principle of Expediency, understood as the consequentialist principle that we should always act so as to bring about the greatest amount of what has intrinsic value. Further, it indicates that, though these are distinct principles, Mill himself always took it for granted that axiological considerations translate ultimately into practical reasons. Honderich's challenge must, then, be met squarely. For, even if there were no relations of entailment or implication between the axiological principle and the consequentialist principle in Mill, there can be no doubt that he held to them both. In this he differed not at all from his classical utilitarian ancestry, who all combined the consequentialist doctrine about what is to be done with a hedonist or welfarist view of what has value. As I shall try to show when I come to consider Mill's theory of the higher and lower pleasures, he did not (as is sometimes suggested) abandon hedonism or welfarism for an early version of ideal utilitarianism similar to that defended by Moore. Rather, Mill enriched the utilitarian tradition by relating its account of practical reasoning to a distinctive theory of morality and by working out a more complex and plausible conception of happiness. What needs to be shown now is that Mill's doctrine of the Art of Life is a legitimate development of the theory of action to which he subscribed, and, more particularly, that Mill is correct in thinking that a morality which is maximally permissive with respect to liberty will be maximally productive of happiness.

How, then, does Mill's argument proceed? In the last chapter of *Utilitarianism*, whose saliency to *On Liberty* has so long been neglected, Mill presents morality as a branch of utility and justice as a branch of morality. In exposition of this account, Mill contends that questions of value must be distinguished from questions of right or wrong, which in turn must be distinguished from questions of justice and injustice. His point is that we cannot always say that a man does wrong when he fails to do what he ought to do; and, even where what a man does is wrong, it need not be unjust. As he puts it:[13]

> We do not call anything wrong, unless we mean to imply that a person ought to be punished in some way or other for doing it; if not by law, by the opinion of his fellow creatures; if not by opinion, by the reproaches of his own conscience. This seems the real turning point of the distinction between morality and simple expediency. It is a part of the notion of Duty in every one of its forms, that a person may rightfully be compelled to fulfil it. Duty is a thing which may be *exacted* from a person, as one exacts a debt. Unless we think that it may be exacted from him, we do not call it his duty. Reasons of prudence, or the interests of other people, may militate against actually exacting it; but the person himself, it is clearly understood, would not be entitled to complain. There are other things, on the contrary, which we wish that people should do, which we like or admire them for doing, perhaps dislike or despise them for not doing, but yet admit that they are not bound to do; it is not a case of moral obligation; we do not blame them, that is, we do not think that they are proper objects of punishment.

In the section immediately preceding this passage, in which a conceptual connection between moral duty and enforceability is emphasised, Mill observes that nothing has as yet been identified which distinguishes the idea of justice from that of moral obligation in general. Where questions of justice are at issue, he asserts, we speak not just of right and wrong actions, but of rights and wrongs — a distinct subject-matter. There are lacunae in Mill's theory, to be sure, but they do not affect his main contentions. For example, it is unclear how Mill wishes to classify supererogatory acts — acts which, though praiseworthy, are not morally obligatory. Does he want to interpret the category of morality so that it includes such acts as morally praiseworthy, or does he want to consign them to the department of excellence? Does Mill wish to identify the morally obligatory and the morally right action? I will not try to answer these questions, since they do not bear on my main argument and Mill's writings do not in any case permit an unequivocal answer to them. A more substantial question concerns the status of the Principle of Utility itself. I have contended that, when taken in conjunction with Expediency, Utility does yield conclusions about what ought to be done. Further, the fact that Utility applies in all the departments of the Art of Life shows strictly, not that it is not a ʿnoral principle, but only that it cannot be *only* a moral principle. ʿnally, Mill himself allows that it is Utility that must settle the issue in ʿʾose cases of extremity where the maxims of the various departments conflict with one another, thereby allowing that Utility-Expediency may serve as practical principles at least in such cases. I do not think that any of these objections show that Utility must in Mill's argument be treated as if it was a moral principle. That Utility may in some cases be invoked to settle practical conflicts does not by itself show it to be a moral principle any more than the fact that it applies within the department of morality shows it to be such. Above all, the fact that Utility and Expediency taken together yield as a theorem the judgment that the act which produces as much happiness as any other ought to be done does not show that Utility and Expediency together frame a moral principle. For nothing said so far tells us anything of Mill's criterion of morally right conduct, which (as I shall later show) is certainly not identified by Mill with maximally expedient conduct. In Mill's own conception of morality, indeed, in which it is necessarily connected with punishability, Utility cannot be a moral principle. Given these considerations, my conclusion stands that Utility in Mill's view of it governs all the areas of the Art of Life, not just morality, and never acquires the character of a moral principle.

Mill's theory of morality and practical reasoning may be summarised thus far: while he recognises utility as the supreme test of all conduct, he affirms that questions of utility and of morality must be distinguished. Because utility does not of itself impose moral requirements upon action, it is mistaken to think that a man must do wrong when he fails to maximise it. Mill's argument in support of the distinction between utility and morality has several layers. In part it proceeds by way of an analysis of the principal moral notions, which presupposes neither utilitarianism nor any other substantive moral theory. In *Utilitarianism* he also argues, more positively, that an act cannot be shown to be wrong unless the institution of some sanction against it can be justified utilitarianly. Inasmuch as any legal or social restraint may be presumed to entail some disutility, there is, after all, a standing utilitarian reason against restraint. Given the connection between moral duty and enforcement, Mill may regret and deplore failures to maximise utility without condemning them as moral failures. In this his theory of morality resembles Hume's account of the artificial virtues in that it contains a utilitarian rationale for the protection of an area of moral indifference. Mill's account of moral rights and of the obligations of justice contains a recognition that direct appeals to utility may even be self-defeating. His discussion in the last chapter of *Utilitarianism* echoes Hume and anticipates later writers[14] in suggesting that a concern for best consequences may dictate support for legal institutions and moral practices which constrain its direct expression. I return to this argument later.

How, then, is the area of moral obligation to be determined? First of all, by applying the Principle of Expediency to the question of enforcement and punishability. That an act is maximally expedient is not, according to Mill, sufficient to show that it would be morally right or obligatory to do it: it must also be true that it is maximally expedient to punish that act's non-performance. It is not the Principle of Expediency alone which gives us Mill's criterion of right conduct, then, but only expediency taken together with his theory of morality as primarily or centrally to do with enforcement and punishment. It is worth noting that revisionary interpreters differ here as to whether Mill's theory of morality is 'act' or 'rule' utilitarian. In part, this controversy is a disagreement as to how the theory of the Art of Life is to be assessed. Is it primarily intended by Mill as an elucidatory exercise, a piece of conceptual analysis, or is it a revisionary proposal about how the term 'morality' is to be used? These questions cannot be answered until the bearing of Mill's distinction between expediency and morality on the structure of his utilitarianism has been properly assessed.

2 ACTS, RULES AND THE ART OF LIFE

Earlier in my exposition of the revisionary interpretation of Mill on liberty, utility and morality, I mentioned his Principle of Expediency, nowhere named as such by Mill, but taken for granted by him and constantly invoked by him in the context of his more detailed discussions. Provisionally, at any rate, the expediency principle may be stated as enjoining that that act ought to be done which produces at least as much of utility as any alternative act. I think it cannot be denied that, whether or not Mill fully distinguished this principle from his Principle of Utility, he is committed to it as providing the criterion of what ought to be done in all areas of life. Unlike the Principle of

Utility, which figures as a principle of evaluation for all states of affairs regardless of whether or not human actions can affect them, this is a principle about action. As such, however, the Principle of Expediency may appear to undermine some of my central claims about the Art of Life. For it seems to import a maximising element into the pursuit of utility which nullifies much of what Mill wants to say about the desirability of its indirect pursuit and about the importance of moral rules in that connection. How, then, can Mill avoid falling on one or other side of the traditional dichotomy of a maximising act-utilitarianism, in which that act is right which produces at least as much good as any available alternative, and some version of rule-utilitarianism (in which an act's rightness is assessed with reference to a utility-promoting rule)?

A number of points need making here. First, the Principle of Expediency, as I have stated it and as I believe Mill would have accepted it, says nothing about the rightness of actions. What it says has as its subject matter the more inclusive category, 'what ought to be done'. It does not mention rightness, let alone moral right and wrong. In fact, as I have already intimated, Mill's criterion of right conduct is wholly distinct from the Principle of Expediency, even though that principle is among the principles which yield the criterion of right conduct. Second, we ought not to neglect the difficulties and implausibilities of taking the Principle of Expediency as being in whole or (in conjunction with the Principle of Utility) a part of a criterion of right conduct. It is obvious to us, as it was to Mill, that we rarely, if ever, know what is the most utility-producing action, and that, even if we do sometimes stumble upon that action, it happens by accident. For all we can know, then, we never do the right action as that would be understood, if the expediency principle were its criterion. There is a massive implausibility in attributing such an understanding of the expediency principle to Mill, given his strong insistence on the limitation and fallibility of all that we take for knowledge.

We recur, then, to the formulation I offered at the end of the last section of this chapter. Not its maximal expediency alone, but only its maximal expediency plus the maximal expediency of making the failure to do it punishable shows an act to be morally right. At this point, however, it may be protested that this makes Mill a rule-utilitarian after all: for is not punishment a matter of rules and of sanctions imposed for their violation? Again, a number of interpreters[15] have pointed to Mill's talk of the tendencies of acts as conclusive evidence in support of a rule-utilitarian interpretation of his moral theory. If, as seems reasonable, we can speak of the tendencies of a class of acts, but not of individual acts, and if Mill's criterion of right conduct requires reference to the tendencies of acts, a rule-utilitarian interpretation would seem to be vindicated.

This is a weak argument, however, for several reasons. When Mill speaks of punishment, he intends not only some sanction imposed (by law or public opinion) by agencies external to the agent who is to be punished: he refers also, and crucially, to the internal disapprobation of conscience. This and other features of Mill's account of punishment show that his criterion of right conduct presupposes a whole moral code, with all its attendant sentiments and attitudes, and not just a set of moral rules. The rightness of an act is not given by its maximal expediency alone, or even by its maximal expediency together with the maximal expediency of instituting a moral or legal rule requiring that it be done, but only by its maximal expediency together with the maximal expediency of making non-compliance punishable by the whole corpus of moral convention and sentiment.

Second, it is an error to suppose that a rule-utilitarian interpretation of Mill's theory is forced on us by his use of the language of tendencies. Such language was used by his father, by Bentham and by John Austin and is in fact typical language in the discussion of these matters by nineteenth-century English-speaking utilitarians. All that it designates, so far as I can see, are the causal powers or properties of acts, which may be very diverse, and which may or may not be statable by us in causal laws. Mill's precepts of art, his axiomata media or secondary maxims are based upon the tendencies of acts inasmuch as they trade upon causal claims about them, but there is no presumption in Mill's moral theory that an act is to be performed simply in virtue of its being the sort required by a precept of art. In a letter quoted by several of his recent interpreters,[16] Mill himself made it unequivocally clear that the classification of acts as to their tendencies was for him only an indispensably useful device in framing precepts of art and not any direct means to judgments about right action. Mill's talk of tendencies of acts does not show that he was a rule-utilitarian, nor even that he was not an act-utilitarian.

If we can ascertain Mill's criterion of wrong conduct, the question of whether he is an act- or a rule-utilitarian, or something else again, will settle itself. Here we ought to recall Mill's explicit statement quoted earlier:[17]

We do not call anything wrong, unless we mean to imply that a
person ought to be punished in some way or other for doing it; if
not by law, by the opinion of his fellow-creatures; if not by opinion,
by the reproaches of his own conscience. This seems the real turning
point of the distinction between morality and simple expediency.

This quotation yields at least in formal terms the framework of
Mill's criterion of wrong conduct. It establishes, first of all, that Mill
cannot be an act-utilitarian. For, according to act-utilitarianism, it is a
necessary and sufficient condition of an act's being wrong that there be
a better alternative to it, so that, on this act-utilitarian view, that act
is right which has best consequences. Mill cannot be an act-utilitarian,
since in his view the fact that an act does not have best consequences is
neither a necessary nor a sufficient condition of its being wrong; the
necessary and sufficient condition of its wrongness is that punishing it
has best consequences. For Mill, then, right acts are a sub-class of
maximally expedient acts, but a wrong act might be maximally expedient. (This is because it might be maximally expedient to do something
which it is maximally expedient be made the object of general dis-
approval or punishment by public opinion.) Mill's crucial distinction,
then, is between acts that are maximally expedient and acts that are
morally required. But taking this distinction seriously, in the way Mill
intended, shows that Mill is not a rule-utilitarian either. For, whereas
for a rule-utilitarian it is a necessary and sufficient condition of an act's
wrongness that it violate a rule whose general observance will have best
consequences, this is not so for Mill. For Mill, the statement of the
necessary and sufficient conditions of moral wrongness need not even
mention social rules. It is necessary and sufficient for the moral wrongness of an act that its disfavouring by public sentiment, the inculcation
of a diposition to avoid it and of a tendency to feel remorse in respect
of its performance, be maximally expedient. No doubt social rules
will be part of any moral code, and an act will be shown to be morally
wrong if a social rule can be instituted against it and that rule has best
consequences if it is generally observed. But a moral code is far more
than a set of social rules, and the prohibition of an act by a social rule
is not a necessary condition of its moral wrongness (though it may be
a sufficient condition thereof). The larger part of any moral code has
to do, not with the institution or enforcement of social rules, but with
the inculcation of sentiments and attitudes and the instilling of dispositions and inclinations. It is to this part of morality, and not to

social rules, that Mill refers, when he speaks of disapprobation by conscience as a crucially important sanction. It is not denied that social rules, like individual acts, may have utility or felicificity for Mill in so far as they tend to promote happiness. But they are not alone in having the property of felicificity, and Mill indeed seems to think that the inculcation of motives and dispositions is more important to the promotion of utility than either the performance of acts or the institution of rules.

Mill's denial that utility, or its action-guiding corollary, expediency, has any direct application to the wrongness of acts, disqualifies the act-utilitarian interpretation of his moral theory, whereas the rule-utilitarian account is disqualified by its unacceptably restrictive emphasis on the institution of social rules in the production of good consequences. Further, both of the standard forms of utilitarianism have difficulty (to put it no more strongly) in coping with the fact that the Art of Life as a whole is intended by Mill to guarantee a large area of moral indifference — an area where moral right and wrong are simply inapplicable. Finally, it may be worth pointing out that both standard forms of utilitarianism tend to be expressed typically in terms of rightness and wrongness. Thus, for an act-utilitarian, that act is right which produces at least as much good as any other, while for a rule-utilitarian an act is right if it conforms with a social rule whose general observance has best consequences. (I ignore here some rival forms of rule-utilitarianism, in which rightness is differently identified, as having only a peripheral relevance to my main argument.) Outside the narrow sphere of morality, however, the precepts of Mill's Art of Life need not mention rightness or wrongness at all. In the areas of prudence and nobility, for example, acts might be assessed as being more or less wise or admirable, without any presumption being made that the wisest or the noblest act available to the agent is the right act. The precepts of nobility and prudence, like those of the larger part of morality, will be efficacious so long as men have a steady inclination to be guided by them. Social rules prescribing or prohibiting actions have only a very limited place in the Art of Life as a whole.

These points may be illustrated by considering briefly Urmson's justly celebrated paper on the interpretation of Mill's moral philosophy, in which a rule-utilitarian interpretation is ably defended. Urmson states Mill's theory of morality in four propositions:[18]

A. A particular action is justified as being right by showing that it

is in accord with some moral rule. It is shown to be wrong by showing that it transgresses some moral rule.

B. A moral rule is shown to be correct by showing that the recognition of that rule promotes the ultimate end.

C. Moral rules can be justified only in regard to matters in which the
general welfare is more than negligibly affected.

D. Where no moral rule is applicable the question of the rightness or
wrongness of particular acts does not arise, though the worth of the
actions can be estimated in other ways.

Here I wish to comment that, whereas propositions B and C are
clearly warranted, I can see no support in Mill's text for propositions
A and D. Mill speaks explicitly of rules being constitutive of morality
only in that sub-department of morality concerning *justice*:[19]

> Justice is a name for certain classes of moral rules, which concern
> the essentials of human well-being more nearly, and are therefore of
> more absolute obligation, than any other rules for the guidance of
> life; and the notion which we have found to be of the essence of the
> idea of justice, that of a right residing in an individual, implies and
> testifies to this more binding obligation.

Elsewhere, though Mill speaks of punishment, of secondary maxims
and so on, he does not specifically mention rules. Thus Urmson tells us
that 'The applicability of moral rules is, says Mill, "the characteristic
difference which marks off, not justice, but morality in general, from
the remaining provinces of Expediency and Worthiness" ' (p. 46 [of the
Everyman edition of *Utilitarianism*]). In the paragraph preceding the
passage Urmson quotes,[20] however, I can find no mention of rules, but
only of fitness or deservingness for punishment and its connections
with moral obligation. As Mill says:[21]

> How we come by these ideas of deserving and not deserving punish-
> ment, will appear, perhaps, in the sequel; but I think there is no
> doubt that this distinction lies at the bottom of the notion of right
> and wrong; that we call any conduct wrong, or employ instead, some
> other term of dislike or disparagement, according as we say that the
> person ought, or ought not, to be punished for it; and we say, it
> would be right to do so, or merely that it would be desirable or
> laudable, according as we would wish to see the person whom it
> concerns, compelled, or only persuaded and exhorted, to act in
> that manner.

It is to punishability, then, not to the institution of a moral rule, that Mill's criteria for moral rightness and wrongness refer and it is accordingly in such terms that propositions A and D are instead to be formulated.

Finally, a point of clarification may be made which illuminates a deep difference between Mill's view of morality and that of at least some rule-utilitarians. Mill never thought it a sufficient or even a necessary condition of the rightness of an act that we can state a rule under which it falls whose general observance would be optimally felicific. Such a reference to hypothetical or ideal moral rules has no part in Mill's utilitarian theory of morality, in which moral rules have little or no weight unless they are embodied in the real social world or can plausibly be instituted there. Again, Mill argued for a strong presumption that the rules which currently prevail in society embody a body of experience greater than any individual can encompass and are not lightly to be abandoned or modified on the basis of our utility calculations alone. In respect of moral rules, one may say, Mill was a Coleridgean utilitarian, but that is not to say that the existence of a rule in the real social world was ever taken by Mill to be sufficient to warrant conformity with it. The fact is that Mill's indirect utilitarianism has no exact fit with either 'ideal-rule' or 'actual-rule' versions of rule-utilitarianism. I conclude that, whereas Urmson's paper succeeds in showing that Mill was not an act-utilitarian, it does not give convincing argument for the claim that he was a rule-utilitarian of any currently recognisable sort. We will profit most, I suggest, if we adopt Urmson's telling critique of the act-utilitarian interpretation of Mill's moral theory, while dropping his unsupported claim that Mill's theory of morality and of practical reasoning must or even does as a matter of fact accord a central place to the institution of rules.

Several questions suggest themselves at once, however. First, we need to ask again, just how is expediency marked off from morality in Mill's account? Plainly, it is an implication of the Principle of Expediency that I have advanced that the utilitarian agent ought to do that act which has best consequences: but what happens to this pure deliberative 'ought' when a utilitarian moral code has been instituted? Second, what is the connection between Mill's formal criterion of wrongness (in terms of the maximal expediency of punishability) and the material criterion – the liberty principle – which Mill advances in *On Liberty*? And, lastly, why specifically does Mill think it self-defeating to appeal directly to expediency when we are to decide practical questions?

Taking these questions in reverse order will enable us to see the complex connections between them. In answer to the last of them, it is important to note that Mill sees a direct appeal to expediency as both individually and collectively self-defeating. It is individually self-defeating, in part because typically we lack the information and the ability to detect the act with best consequences, and in part because happiness is not for men something that can be achieved directly. The latter point depends on Mill's complex post-Benthamite moral psychology, in which it is recognised that human happiness is achieved not in the passive experience of any specific sensation, but in the successful pursuit of ends valued in themselves. One might almost say that, for Mill, the idea that an individual could directly pursue his own happiness involves a sort of category mistake or at least a psychological paradox. Mill gives explicit expression to his conviction that the pursuit in any direct way of one's own happiness is self-defeating in his *Autobiography*. Speaking of the 'very marked effects' on his opinions and character wrought by the mental crisis he suffered in early manhood, Mill observes:

> I never, indeed, wavered in the conviction that happiness is the test of all rules of conduct, and the end of life. But I now thought that this end was only to be attained by not making it the direct end. Those only are happy (I thought) who have their minds fixed on some object other than their happiness; on the happiness of others, on the improvement of mankind, even on some art or pursuit, followed not as a means, but as itself an ideal end.

For Mill, indeed, as I shall later try to show, these pursuits and ideals taken up independently of their contribution to one's own happiness actually figure as ingredients of happiness as he conceives of it.[22]

The direct pursuit of happiness is supposed by Mill to be collectively self-defeating, partly once again in virtue of the lack of any dependable test which identifies the best act, but also in virtue of certain indispensable conditions or terms of social co-operation. I will try to sort out what these are when I come in the next chapter to discuss the Principle of Liberty as a principle of social co-operation, but it may suffice here to say that, for Mill, any principle is disqualified as a guide for setting the terms of social co-operation if it fails to protect men's vital interests. For Mill, crucially, protection of these vital interests has itself a utilitarian rationale acknowledged in his theory of justice.

Filling out the connections between the formal and the material elements of Mill's criterion of wrong conduct mainly involves spelling

out points I have already made. One hinge of Mill's argument is his conceptual analysis of wrongness, already mentioned, in which it is necessarily connected with punishability. This is backed up in the relevant
passages from *Utilitarianism* by what can best be called an excursion
into the natural history of morality. Mill sees the ground of moral feeling, and especially of the sense of justice, in the sentiment, not itself
moral, in which we seek retaliation for injury to our interests and, by
an extension of sympathy which Mill thinks natural to man, for injury
to the interests of other members of the society of which we form a
part. As Mill puts it: 'The sentiment of justice ... is thus, I conceive,
the natural feeling of retaliation or vengeance, rendered by intellect and
sympathy applicable to those injuries, that is, to those hurts, which
wound us through, or in common with, society at large.'[23] Here Mill
advances a conception of morality as collective self-defence in which
the sense of justice has a paramount place. It is not a fair description
to call this a piece of conceptual analysis, though other aspects of Mill's
argument, such as his assertion of a necessary connection between
wrongness and punishability, involve an analysis of moral notions.
Rather, Mill is engaging in speculative moral sociology of a historical
sort to conjecture what are the social uses or natural functions of moral
sentiment. When Mill then goes on to argue from the conception of
morality as collective self-defence to the liberty principle, he trades on
these speculative propositions in moral sociology at least in so far as
he assumes that self-defence is the primitive source of moral sentiment
in natural feeling.

We are now at a point in our inquiry at which we can confront what
is, perhaps, the most obvious as well as the most formidable difficulty
for Mill's account of the relations of morality with expediency. Earlier
I asked what became of the 'ought' of expediency when once a utilitarian moral code has been established. The question has been put,
more forcefully but entirely fairly, by Ten in his recent book, when he
asks how Mill is to cope with a collision of the demands of morality
with those of expediency. He concludes:[24]

There is nothing in Mill's analysis of the concept of morality to show
that the requirements of morality must take precedence over all non-
moral considerations . . . . Thus we may not have a moral obligation
always to maximise happiness, but from this alone it does not follow
that we should not always act to maximise happiness even when this
involves the violation of our moral obligations.

36

As Ten acknowledges, an attempt to answer this criticism has been made by a number of recent writers, of whom the most noteworthy are Rolf Sartorius and R. M. Hare. Sartorius has argued that even the classical act-utilitarian can give some independent weight to moral norms as follows:[25]

> The act-utilitarian is therefore in fact able to give an account of social norms which bar direct appeals to utility as more than mere rules of thumb in a two-fold sense. Firstly, they perform the central function of directing human behaviour into channels that it would not otherwise take by restructuring the sets of considerations of consequences of which utilitarian moral agents must take account. Secondly, they provide reasons for action in that their conventional acceptance is tantamount to the existence of systems of warranted expectations the disappointment of which is a disutility according to standard or normal cases of their violation.

Ten is not satisfied with these arguments. He holds against Sartorius that, even if utilitarian arguments could support the institution of absolute moral rules, these need not and often would not have a liberal content, and he gives James Fitzjames Stephen as an example of a consistent utilitarian who accords great weight to moral rules but denies that these rules ought on utilitarian grounds to have any special tenderness to liberty.[26] Again, discussing R. M. Hare's proposal that different levels of moral thought may be distinguished in such a way that moral norms may consistently with the demands of utility be accorded a weight greater than rules of thumb, Ten advances as 'a fatal flaw'[27] in any interpretation of Mill on these lines that it would result in a hardening of attitude to moral precepts (including the Principle of Liberty) which is wholly at odds with Mill's general opposition to prejudice and moral sentiment unsupported by reason.

I do not see that these criticisms have the force Ten attributes to them. It is true that, like other moral reformers, Mill is committed to seeking a point of balance between the practice of moral criticism and the preservation of existing moral life. But, though he was always opposed to intuitionism and appeal to sentiment as elements in a theory of moral knowledge, Mill nowhere denied the importance to a free society of stable moral sentiments and of spontaneous moral responses. The balance Mill seeks is no doubt a delicate one, but there seems nothing absurd in his ideal of a form of moral life in which utilitarianly sanctioned precepts are accorded great weight and yet remain open to question and challenge. In short, I cannot see that Ten has shown Hare's proposal about levels of moral thought to be a psychological or a sociological impossibility, or that it fails to square with Mill's attitude to ordinary moral life.

With regard to Sartorius's attempt to give a utilitarian justification of the institution of 'absolute' moral norms, Ten fails to give full weight to the distinction I have already mentioned between the formal and the material aspects of Mill's criterion of wrong conduct. The key claim of Sartorius's argument is in fact the formal thesis that there is nothing in utilitarianism against (and there may be utilitarian reasons in favour of) according moral norms absolute or quasi-absolute status. For the argument that such rules would have a liberal content we need to turn to Mill's theory of happiness and his conception of the vital interests. Without these elements of Mill's theory, it would indeed be consistent to argue (as Ten and Fitzjames Stephen do) against Mill and Sartorius that giving a due utilitarian weight to existing sentiments will often yield illiberal maxims. This is a point to which I shall return in the next chapter.

Ten's most fundamental objection to the reinterpretation of Mill advanced by the revisionary writers is that it does not account for the priority of moral over other practical considerations or show why morality should not yield when it comes into competition with expediency. This is, I think, the same point, stated in other terms, as Honderich makes when he contends[28] that the Principle of Liberty must either be the Principle of Utility at another remove, or else unjustifiable in utilitarian terms. In both Ten and Honderich, the objection being put is that moral norms cannot be derived from utility which are then exempt from utilitarian overriding. It will be my argument, however, that this derivation is just what must follow if Mill is right in his belief that direct appeal to utility is in various ways self-defeating. On this view, moral norms *must* have a weight independent of their direct utility, if they are to be maximally efficacious in promoting utility. I will try to support this thesis of Mill's about the self-defeating effect of direct utilitarianism in the next chapter.

The upshot of my argument so far is that I attribute to Mill a species of utilitarian moral theory, distinct from act- and rule-utilitarianism, which (following some recent writers)[29] I shall call *indirect utilitarianism*. What are the distinctive features of Mill's indirect utilitarianism? I suggest they are two: first, that neither the general happiness nor the agent's own happiness is to be the object of direct pursuit; and second, that utility, in conjunction with its action-guiding corollary, expediency, serves as a principle of evaluation of whole systems of precepts of art, among which moral codes have central (but not exclusive) interest. My aim is to suggest the power and plausibility of Mill's indirect utilitarian derivation of important precepts of art, such as the Principle of Liberty, and its consilience with a more general utilitarian account of justice and the moral rights.

It will be apparent that, in this interpretation of Mill, morality is viewed as an important social instrument concerned with the utility-maximising co-ordination of human activities. Some may find such an externalist and instrumental conception of morality problematic inasmuch as it seems to produce a bifurcation between the standpoints of the utilitarian moral agent and of the utilitarian ideal observer. One can easily imagine such a bifurcation coming about when one realises that, in Mill's utilitarian society, an agent might be required by utility to perform acts which the utilitarianly sanctioned moral practices in which he participates merely allow. Inasmuch as the area of liberty surrounding a moral practice is for Mill an area of moral indifference, how is the individual to decide what to do? In part, no doubt, Mill would follow Bentham in this area — as he does in much of the doctrine of the Art of Life. Applying Bentham's differently formulated but substantially similar distinction between public and private ethics, Mill would maintain that utility will generally be promoted if, in the private or self-regarding sphere, men consult prudence and worthiness. To this it will doubtless be objected that, while consulting prudence and worthiness in the area of moral indifference may as a generalisation promote utility, it need not and will not do so in every instance. It might still be true that, utilitarianly speaking, a man ought to do what he has no utilitarianly sanctioned obligation to do. Resistance to this aspect of Mill's argument derives, most probably, from suspicion of an account of morality in which its importance is not categorical but instrumental — but such an account is integral to utilitarianism in any of its forms.

My view is that Mill may consistently allow an important place for moral rules and social norms, which generate obligations and which bar direct appeal to utility, without abandoning his utilitarian commitment. His claim is that all such rules or maxims, including the all-important Principle of Liberty, are derivable from utility even though their role is to disqualify direct appeal to it. It might still be urged that the theory of the Art of Life that I have expounded involves a separation of the viewpoint of the utilitarian observer from that of the moral agent which is puzzling, and to which Mill himself found difficulty in adhering. His difficulties in this connection are evidenced, perhaps, in the uncertainty he displays as to how exactly the departments of the Art of Life are to be distinguished from one another. In *A System of Logic*, Mill speaks of 'the Art of Life, in its three departments, Morality, Prudence or Policy, and Aesthetics; the Right, the Expedient, and the Beautiful or Noble, in human conduct or works'.[30] In the essay on *Bentham*, however, he speaks of action possessing 'a *moral* aspect, that of its *right* or *wrong*; its *aesthetic* aspect, or that of its beauty; its *sympathetic* aspect, or that of its *lovableness*'. 'The first,' he says, 'addresses itself to our reason and conscience; the second to our imagination; the third to our human fellow-feeling.'[31]

In contrast to this classification, in which prudence is left out, we find a third division in *Utilitarianism*, where (as Brown notes) morality is demarcated from the remaining provinces of expediency and worthiness.[32]

Brown has pointed out that Ryan's original account of the Art of Life is unacceptable in that, whereas it differentiates prudence and morality as concerned with the happiness of self and others respectively, morality — in Mill's view and in fact — requires impartiality between self and others. The difficulty for our view of the place of utility in Mill's thought, as Sidgwick discovered when in considering the relations of duty and interest in Mill's thought he was driven (under Butler's influence) to accept a basic 'dualism of practical reason', is that the demands of prudence sometimes conflict with those of morality. If the utility principle contains a requirement of impartiality between the happiness of self and others, is it not then a moral principle? The difficulty is deepened by Mill's claim that, in neglecting the relations between character and action, Bentham had impoverished the idea of morality. As Halliday has put it,[33] 'whatever else was implied by the new ethic of self-culture, the Benthamite understanding of the scope and application of moral judgment was completely inadequate'. The point is clearly made by Ryan in his account of the Art of Life: 'The problem . . . is to square the apparent implications of these distinctions (made in the Art of Life) with Mill's complaints . . . that Bentham had omitted important *moral* considerations in not looking at the relationship between the agent's character and the actions he performs.' 'If morality is held by Mill to be coextensive with the area of duty, and to tell us what we *must* do and what we can properly be compelled to do, then it seems that worthiness comes within the area of compulsion, after all.'[34] We have seen already that, in requiring us to be impartial between our own happiness and that of others, utility begins to look like a moral principle. Now we find Mill bringing aesthetic-looking judgments (judgments of worthiness) about self-development within the moral area.

These uncertainties in Mill's formulation of the Art of Life suggest a difficulty in the indirect utilitarian interpretation I have given of it; how can Mill consistently give importance to the worth of character? How can his utilitarianism be squared with his apparent conviction that human worthiness can and should be appraised without reference to the good states of affairs that it produces? We come again upon the most important feature of Mill's utilitarianism, namely, its indirect character. As Mill himself puts it in *Bentham*: 'We think utility, or happiness, much too complex and indefinite an end to be sought except through the medium of various secondary ends . . . . Those who adopt utility can seldom apply it truly except through the secondary principles.'[35] Mill's conviction, expressed in these and other passages, was that a man became a reliable source of happiness to himself and others, only in so far as he became attached to specific things (projects, activities, persons) for their own sakes. If the direct pursuit of happiness or utility was generally self-defeating, utility required a type of human character formed to value things in and for themselves, and it required the development of a sense of self-esteem or moral dignity by appeal to which a man judged himself and others. It is to standards of nobility or worthiness, then, as well as to moral standards, that a man ought to appeal in the ordinary affairs of life. The apparent paradox of Mill's insistence on the importance of human worthiness to the promotion of happiness is resolved once we grasp that Mill thought utility required that human worthiness, like other good things, ought to be pursued as an end in itself.

Resolving this apparent difficulty in Mill's account of the worth of character may enable us to see our way through some of the broader difficulties about the 'external' or 'instrumental' character of morality in Mill's system. The most distinctive feature of Mill's indirect utilitarianism is found in the separation it introduces between the practical and the critical levels of reasoning about conduct. In Mill's account, precepts of art, whether they be moral or not in content and function, supply the considerations which we are to invoke in our practical deliberations. It is only at the critical level of reasoning about conduct that the Principle of Utility is typically invoked. At the principle level, we are to rely on the considerations built into the various precepts, which give content to the several departments of the Art of Life. Direct appeal to Utility is allowable for Mill only where it is unavoidable, that is, when the precepts of art at our disposal conflict with each other or (perhaps because of the novelty of our circumstances) give no clear guidance. Mill's indirect utilitarianism, then, embraces a hierarchical theory of reasoning about conduct, not only moral conduct, but all branches of practical life. In ordinary circumstances, neither morality nor prudence or nobility will be experienced as 'external' to the agent, since their precepts will have been internalised by him. It is only if one does not grasp the distinction between those considerations which an agent ought to invoke in his practical deliberations and those which ultimately justify his actions that Mill's theory of morality and of practical reasoning in general will seem odd or misconceived.

3 UTILITY, PLEASURE AND HAPPINESS

I trust that I have by now clarified and defended some of the most important formal aspects of Mill's utilitarianism. Even if this part of Mill's doctrine is accepted, we have still to show why it is that happiness alone has value and how happiness is connected with liberty. Before looking at Mill's famous 'proof' of utility, which has had to withstand the scornful dismissal of such figures as G. E. Moore, F. H. Bradley and H. W. B. Joseph,[36] let us be clear in what respects Mill's views differ from those still often attributed to him. As Fred Berger has shown in systematic detail in his important work on Mill,[37] Mill did not subscribe either to psychological hedonism or to psychological egoism: that is to say, he never held that men always act from a desire for pleasure or happiness, whether that pleasure or happiness be their own, or that of all those affected by the actions available to them. His view, rather, was that pleasure and pain are *causally* linked to all voluntary human acts (though sometimes only indirectly, through past associations of the act with pleasure). Evidence in support of the imputation to Mill of this view can be found in his early essay *Remarks on Bentham's Philosophy* (1833), in the later and more famous essay on *Bentham* (1838), and in the footnote he added to his 1869 edition of his father's *Analysis of the Phenomena of the Human Mind*. Most importantly, though, in view of the extent to which Mill's views have been misunderstood and misrepresented, he explicitly rejects the view that men always or typically act from a desire for pleasure in his immensely influential *System of Logic*, saying:[38]

> When the will is said to be determined by motives, a motive does not mean always, or solely, the anticipation of a pleasure or of a pain . . . . It is only when our purposes have become independent of the feelings of pain or pleasure from which they originally took their rise that we are said to have a confirmed character.

Again, far from holding that each man always seeks his own pleasure or good, Mill frequently and insistently asserts that many pains and pleasures are essentially sympathetic or altruistic in character. In a footnote which he appended to his edition of his father's *Analysis*,[39] he observes:

> It is evident, that the only pleasures or pains of which we have direct experience being those felt by ourselves, it is from them that our very notions of pleasure and pain are derived. It is also obvious that the pleasure or pain with which we contemplate the pleasure or pain felt by someone else, is itself a pleasure or pain of our own. But if it be meant that in such cases the pleasure or pain is consciously referred to self, I take this to be mistaken.

Mill's view, then, is not that men always act from a desire for pleasure, their own or that of others, but that the desires for the sake of which they act are causally related by association with ideas of pleasure or pain. It is because this is his view that in *Utilitarianism* Mill is able consistently to maintain that men may desire things apart from pleasure, and desire these things for their own sakes. As he puts it:[40]

> Whatever is desired otherwise than as a means to some end beyond itself, and ultimately to happiness, is desired as itself a part of happiness, and is not desired for itself until it has become so. Those who desire virtue for its own sake, desire it either because the consciousness of it is a pleasure, or because the consciousness of being without it is a pain, or for both reasons united.

Here Mill's claim is that things other than pleasure may be desired for their own sakes, and that, being desired for their own sakes, they are to be accounted components of happiness which, as he puts it, is 'not an abstract idea, but a concrete whole'.[41] It was Mill's view, indeed, that happiness is likely to be achieved not by way of the direct pursuit of pleasure, but rather by the pursuit of things other than pleasure, by involvement in activities and projects which are valued for their own sakes. It is here that one must avoid a misunderstanding of Mill, suggested by Dryer's account. Dryer correctly points out that, though Mill describes his happiness principle as the 'sole criterion' for the assessment of conduct, this does not imply that the only way by which anyone can know whether a certain action should be done is by seeking to make out whether it would cause more happiness than any alternative: as Dryer puts it, 'Mill's principle does not supply the only test; it only lays down a condition to which any test must comply.'[42] If I understand his view correctly, however, Dryer is in error when he goes on to say of the utility principle that[43]

> It implies that no human being or human disposition is desirable or undesirable for its own sake. According to it, the only sort of matter that is desirable or undesirable for its own sake is a state of affairs comprising sentient beings. It implies that neither justice nor liberty nor peace is desirable for its own sake.

The view expressed in the last sentence I have quoted is in error, since, if happiness is the only thing desirable for its own sake, there will be many things desirable for their own sakes in virtue of their being necessary ingredients of happiness. Further, if happiness contains things desired for their own sakes apart from pleasure, then happiness and pleasure have been distinguished in Mill's account. In this case, however, it is open to Mill to contend that some kinds of pleasure are more valuable than others, inasmuch as they make a greater contribution to happiness. I will return to this point, when in chapter 4 I relate Mill's conception of happiness together with his account of the higher and lower pleasures to his theory of individuality.

At this point in my exposition it may reasonably be objected that, however Mill conceives of happiness, he has not shown that it is the only thing that is ultimately valuable. Now I do not want here to undertake a systematic discussion of Mill's 'proof', but it may be worth making some fairly uncontroversial observations at this point. First, as should be suggested by Mill's well-known remarks that 'ultimate ends do not admit of proof, in the ordinary acceptation of the term', though 'considerations may be presented capable of determining the intellect either to give or withhold its assent',[44] Mill did not suppose he was offering any sort of rigorously demonstrative argument in support of the claim that only happiness (with its necessary ingredients) has intrinsic value. Nor, second, did he commit a fallacy of naturalism, if by that is meant a species of definist fallacy. Mill does not claim that 'being desirable' is synonymous or interdefinable with 'being desired' or 'being capable of being desired'. His argument is, rather, that only things which are capable of being desired can be intrinsically desirable, and, further, that the fact that something is desired is evidence that it is desirable. While these arguments may endorse a theory of value that is, in some senses of the term, 'naturalistic', and while there may be important criticisms to be made of any such theory, it should be perfectly plain that nowhere does Mill seek to define intrinsic desirability in terms of capability of being desired. So Mill does not commit a fallacy of equivocation in this portion of his arguments. Nor, third, and finally, does he commit a fallacy of composition. In a letter to a correspondent, Mill explicitly disavows any such compositional move: 'When I said that the general happiness is a good to the aggregate of all persons, I did not mean that every human being's happiness is a good to every other human being.'[45]

Let us suppose, then, that Mill has given reason in support of his claim that only happiness has intrinsic value. What is the connection between happiness and liberty? At this point I wish to present merely a sketch of Mill's argument, which will be analysed in greater detail in chapter 4.

Mill's departures from the classical utilitarian view of human nature, which he criticises so sharply in his *Bentham* and *Coleridge*, support the Doctrine of Liberty in at least four ways. First, in abandoning the passive conception of the mind which he ascribed to Bentham and his father, Mill embraced a conception of happiness which was Aristotelian in that it was inseparably connected with activity. No longer could a happy human life be conceived of as one containing a number of goods supposed to be enjoyable independently of man's energetic pursuit of them. Second, it was Mill's belief that, once a certain level of social development has been reached, men will find their happiness in activities of which choice or 'individuality' is a necessary ingredient. Whereas Mill does not, as I hope to show, attach to choice-making itself a value independent of its contribution to happiness, he does claim that men are creatures of such a kind that once they have known them, they will not lightly give up the forms of happiness into which choice-making enters as a necessary ingredient. Third, Mill's conception of happiness was avowedly individualist and pluralist. According to Mill, each man possesses a quiddity or peculiar endowment, the development of which is indispensable to his happiness. Fourth, Mill thought of the pursuit of happiness as issuing, not in a Rawls-type rational plan of life, but rather in a series of 'experiments of living',[46] each of which was to be altered successively in view of what had been learnt from the others. For the individual as for the species, this must be conceived of as an open-ended venture. Even where particular experiments are irreversible and disastrous, the liberty to undertake them is necessary if contemporaries and future generations are able to benefit from the knowledge they yield.

Our understanding of Mill's utilitarianism may be assisted if we treat it as having a hierarchical structure. It has at least three distinct tiers. First we have the utility principle in its role as an axiological principle specifying happiness alone as of instrinsic value. The happiness here is that of any sentient creature, jellyfish, lower mammal or human being, with states of mind or feelings or preferences determinate enough for the utility principle to operate upon. Next we have utility in its applications to human beings, whose generic powers allow for happy and wretched lives whose qualities are (so far as we know) peculiar to our species. It is at this level that there come into play those general facts of human nature, contingent in that they might conceivably have been otherwise but unalterable so far as men are concerned, which inform and shape the various precepts of the Art of Life. Third, there are the applications of the utility principle to reflective and civilised men in whom the capacities for an autonomous life have been developed and to whom the higher pleasures are accessible. Here the Doctrine of Liberty itself comes into play. In according a special weight to the higher pleasures, the utility principle in Mill may seem to have an ideal-regarding aspect and to express a sort of procedural perfectionism in which choice-making itself rather than the style of life chosen has intrinsic value. Once the three-tiered structure of Mill's utilitarianism is appreciated, the attribution to his doctrine of a perfectionist aspect[47] may be seen to be quite misleading. It appears to have such an aspect only in its application to men who have attained a certain stage of cultural development. It remains throughout want-regarding[48] in that the third tier of Mill's utilitarianism reposes on the wager that civilised men will in fact prefer the life of free men because it is in such a life that they find their happiness.

Mill's indirect utilitarianism consists in the thesis that, whereas the Principle of Utility supplies the standard of evaluation for all codes of conduct, the direct appeal to Utility to settle practical questions is typically self-defeating. This self-defeatingness of direct utilitarianism is supported, partly by reference to the distinctive characteristics of human happiness and partly by claims about the necessary conditions of stable social co-operation. Also, no doubt, Mill thought any form of direct utilitarianism was disqualified by the great fact of human fallibility. Other variants of indirect utilitarianism are conceivable, supported by reasonings different from Mill's, but all will share with Mill's the thesis that appeal to Utility in the context of practical dilemmas is generally self-defeating and all will issue in a complex and hierarchical theory of practical reasoning. The importance of the hierarchical structure of Mill's utilitarianism is revealed in the fact that at the second level choice-making or autonomy will not enjoy the centrality and priority among man's vital interests that it possesses at the third. It is a criticism of Mill's doctrine of liberty, in fact, that in virtue of the necessary conditions which he specifies in the *Logic* as being indispensable to any stable social order, the third level can never be reached. I will not comment here on this criticism, or on the possibilities of conflict between the three tiers of Mill's utilitarian theory which it may disclose, since I intend to treat some of these criticisms in the last chapter of this book. I will only reiterate my conviction that, unless the indirect and hierarchical character of Mill's utilitarianism, its dependency on Mill's philosophical psychology and its embeddedness in his conception of human nature are fully taken into account, Mill's interpreters and critics will remain puzzled or unconvinced by his argument for the centrality and priority of liberty among the ingredients necessary to the well-being of men of the sort to whom the *Liberty* is addressed. It remains, however, to ascertain just what was the Principle of Liberty which Mill sought to defend in his famous Essay.

III

THE PRINCIPLE OF LIBERTY

1 THE SELF-REGARDING AREA, HARM TO OTHERS AND THE THEORY OF VITAL INTERESTS

When Mill characterised the maxim whose adoption he sought to defend in the *Liberty* as 'one very simple principle',[1] he gave a hostage to fortune. The Principle of Liberty is anything but simple, and controversy continues to flourish as to its force and its place in Mill's Doctrine of Liberty taken as a whole. Mill's own statements are not greatly helpful to his interpreters. Whereas he refers in the *Autobiography*[2] to *On Liberty* as 'a kind of philosophic textbook of a single truth', he speaks in the latter, not just of 'one very simple principle', but of 'two maxims' as its prescriptive content. Apart from the broad question of the relation of his Principle of Liberty to his whole Doctrine of Liberty, which I shall explore in the last section of this chapter, the Principle itself displays an aspect of indeterminacy or ambiguity which I would like to reduce. One area of difficulty in interpreting Mill's Doctrine of Liberty arises from the question whether Mill's principle about liberty is a principle licensing liberty-restriction where harm to others is thereby *prevented*, or a principle of a narrower and more stringent sort, allowing liberty-limitation only in respect of conduct which *causes harm*. Before we can proceed to attempt to clarify that area of obscurity, however, we need to be clear what it is that Mill understands by harm. At once we find ourselves in some difficulty.

The severity of our (and Mill's) difficulties may be gauged by the fact that one writer has gone so far as to assert that the whole argument of *On Liberty* 'is vitiated by the ambiguity in Mill's use of the word "harm" '.[3] Certainly, there are real problems surrounding Mill's use of the term. Does he intend the reader to understand 'harm' to refer only to physical harm, or must a class of moral harms to character be included in any application of the liberty principle? Must the harm that the restriction on liberty prevents be done directly to identifiable individuals, or may it also relevantly be done to institutions, social practices and forms of life? Can serious offence to feelings count as harm so far as the restriction of liberty is concerned, or must the harm be done to interests, or to those interests the protection of which is to be accorded the status of a right? Can a failure to benefit someone, or to perform one's obligations to the public, be construed as a case in which harm has been done? These difficulties express a philosophical difficulty in the analysis of the concept of harm — a difficulty emerging from the fact that judgments about harm are often controversial as between exponents of different moral outlooks. Can a purely naturalistic account of the meaning of 'harm' be accepted as adequate to the demands of ordinary thought and practice? Or, if writers such as Winch[4] are right in thinking that judgments about harm do not occupy some common ground of moral neutrality between differing ways of life, could Mill be warranted in working with a revisionary conception of harm? These are some of the difficulties which suggest themselves naturally to anyone interested in the clarification or application of Mill's Principle of Liberty. For what is the sense or use of a principle telling us that liberty may not be limited save to prevent harm to others if we find ourselves hopelessly at odds over what is to count as 'harm'?

It seems indisputable, then, that, if it is to be at all useful, the liberty principle must be taken as presupposing that there is a domain of human action where what a man does, though it may harm him, is not harmful to others. Ever since *On Liberty* was published, the commonest line of criticism of his argument has been that it presupposes what does not exist — a domain of purely self-regarding actions which non-trivially affect only the agent and no one else. If this is so, then Mill's principle cannot do the job he had in mind for it — that of securing a determinate and important area of human life from liberty-limiting invasion.

One attempt to answer this traditional criticism is made by John Rees in a well-known paper.[5] Rees distinguishes between actions that affect others and actions that affect others' interests, and claims that Mill's working conception of harm is that of harm to interests. Now, according to Rees, 'when a person can be thought to have interests he is thereby possessed of a right', if only the right to have his interests taken into account. Rees emphasises that interests 'depend for their existence on social recognition and are closely connected with prevailing standards about the sort of behaviour a man can legitimately expect from others'.[6] Two points are relevant to Rees's intepretation. First, though he emphasises that neither he nor Mill is saying that rights and interests are synonymous terms, but only that they are very closely related to each other, rights and interests are importantly different in several ways, some of which Mill gives evidence of seeing as relevant to his argument. It is not, perhaps, an entirely trivial point that, whereas a man's interests may be damaged or obstructed by an impersonal process such as a natural catastrophe, his rights can be affected only by the actions of other human beings.[7] True enough, Mill is concerned in *On Liberty* not with all cases where a man's interests are damaged, but only with those where his interests are invaded, that is, damaged by other men. But the fact that these cases can be distinguished shows that there are cases where what we say about a man's interests need have no implications for what we think about his rights. Second, it should be noted that, when in a passage that Rees quotes Mill tries to demarcate the area of life in which he may be held accountable to society, he speaks not of determining what are a man's interests, but of ascertaining his rights. 'This conduct,' he says, 'consists in not injuring the interests of one another: or rather *certain* interests which, either by express legal provision or by tacit understanding, *ought to be considered as rights*.' Here the test is not whether a man's interests have been damaged by other men, but whether his interests ought to be protected as rights.

Mill does not think, then, that if a man has an interest, he 'thereby' has any kind of right. His reference to 'certain interests' suggests that only *some* interests can give rise to rights, but which? In order to distinguish interests from 'arbitrary wishes, fleeting fancies, or capricious demands',[8] Rees stresses their dependence on norms and values which enjoy social recognition. But this is open to the objection (made by Wollheim[9]) that the liberty principle in Rees's interpretation becomes relativistic and conservative in character and cannot perform the critical functions Mill intended for it. The boundaries of the self-regarding domain will be determined by the currently dominant conception of interests, and the liberty principle will expand freedom only in so far as legal limitations on liberty lag behind changing conceptions of human interests. Wollheim's objection to Rees is forceful, if Rees's account may be interpreted as making human interests subordinate to their social recognition; and there can be no doubt that so thoroughly relativistic a conception of interests cannot accord with Mill's intentions. Such relativism can be avoided, however, without making interests wholly invariant socially and historically. Men's interests might be, and indeed must be shaped by the standards and circumstances of their time and culture, but to say this is not to say that men's interests wholly depend upon or are entirely constituted by recognition by society. The liberty principle need not itself be entirely relativistic in character, even if (as must surely be the case) its application is relativistic in some degree. Mill needs a conception of interests that is universalistic inasmuch as it specifies an area essential to human well-being, but which has also a developmental or historical aspect. To affirm that this is what Mill needs – and to argue, as I will go on to do, that this is what his writings contain – is not to lose sight of the vital insight contained in Rees's interpretation, namely, that for Mill an intimate connection did hold between moral rights and 'certain interests'. For Mill, indeed, moral rights are definable, or at least defensible, only in terms of men's primary or essential interests. Fundamental human moral rights are for Mill rights to the protection of these interests by law and moral convention.

What, then, are the 'essential interests' which, according to Mill, are to be protected as moral rights, once certain conditions have been satisfied? In *Utilitarianism* Mill asserts:

> The moral rules which forbid mankind to hurt one another (in which we must never forget to include wrongful interference with each other's freedom) are more vital to human well-being than any maxims, however important, which only point out the best mode of managing some department of human affairs.

He goes on to assert that:

> the moralities which protect every individual from being harmed by others, either directly or by being hindered in his freedom of pursuing his own good, are at once those which he himself has most at heart, and those which he has the strongest interest in publishing and enforcing by word and deed . . . it is these moralities primarily which compose the obligations of justice.

Mill continues by affirming that:

51

the most marked cases of injustice . . . are acts of wrongful aggression, or wrongful exercise of power over some one; the next are those which consist in wrongfully withholding from him something which is his due; in both cases, inflicting on him a positive hurt, either in the form of direct suffering, or of the privation of some good which he had reasonable ground, either of a physical or of a social kind, for counting upon.

He concludes by observing summarily that: 'justice is a name for certain moral requirements, which regarded collectively, stand higher in the scale of social utility, and are therefore of more paramount obligation, than any others'.[10]

Mill here identifies as man's most vital interests his interests in autonomy and in security. The significance of this claim for the argument of *On Liberty* can scarcely be exaggerated. These are the 'certain interests' which Mill there specifies are to be protected as rights. Except in certain contractual circumstances where special rights exist, and in certain circumstances of emergency,[11] these interests are satisfied when men refrain from invading one another's autonomy and from undermining one another's security. Unless these vital interests are endangered, no policy which aims at preventing men from harming themselves, or at compelling them to benefit others, can ever be justified. It is to these interests that Mill refers in the introductory chapter of *On Liberty* when he makes the appeal to 'the permanent interests of man as a progressive being' and which function in Mill's theory of liberty in a fashion analogous to that of the primary goods in Rawls's theory of justice. These vital interests are to be protected before any others a man may have; and they are not to be invaded or damaged simply because it seems that a greater satisfaction of overall preferences might thereby be achieved. Mill argues to this effect in his *Auguste Comte and Positivism*, asserting that 'It is incumbent on everyone to restrain the pursuit of his personal objects within the limits consistent with the essential interests of others.'[12] That Mill does work with a theory of essential or vital interests cannot reasonably be doubted. It might still be objected that nothing has yet been said which supports the contention that these are the interests in security and in autonomy. Still less has it been shown that there are good arguments in Mill for ascribing a priority to the vital interest in autonomy where this conflicts with the demands of security. Until we know Mill's account of the scope and importance of these vital interests, we have not captured the structure of his argument from utility to the Principle of Liberty.

Thus a central difficulty in explicating Mill's theory of the moral rights, and so of identifying the force of the liberty principle, is that of determining what is comprehended within men's vital interests in security and in autonomy. For, unless the domains of these interests can be clearly demarcated from other human interests, the liberty principle will not be able to guide action in the way Mill hoped for it. It might be thought that difficulties about Mill's conception of harm here re-emerge. More radically, when discussing the nature of the demands upon action imposed by the Principle of Utility, I adopted the strategy of assuming for the purposes of my interpretation that Mill's utilitarianism does entail a maximising commitment about utility's promotion. In this I foreswore the alternative strategy of denying that maximisation is either a rational or a moral requirement of a plausible theory of value. We are now able to point to two central obscurities in the logic of Mill's argument for moral rights as I have presented it so far. First, what justifies the weighting of men's vital interests over all men's other interests? How can any theory appealing finally to general welfare resist a trade-off between some interests, however vital, and others, when protecting the latter will yield a net utility benefit? Second, it is not at all clear that we have yet demarcated the vital interests satisfactorily from the others — that is to say, we have not yet framed the self-regarding area in any acceptable way.

Before I go on to try to answer the first of these questions, it may be worth looking again at what may be comprehended in the category of man's essential or permanent interests. I have identified Mill's view of these vital or essential interests as the interests each man has, in Mill's view, in autonomy and in security. But what is encompassed by the interests framed by these terms? With regard to the essential interest in security, we have little difficulty in establishing how Mill wishes us to understand this. Speaking of the 'extraordinarily important and impressive kind of utility which is concerned (in cases where moral rights are threatened)', Mill goes on to specify:[13]

> The interest involved is that of security, to everyone's feelings the most vital of all interests. All other earthly benefits are needed by one person, not needed by another, and many of them can, if necessary, be cheerfully forgone, or replaced by something else, but security no human being can possibly do without; on it we depend for all our immunity from evil, and for the whole value of all and

every good, beyond the passing moment; since nothing but the gratification of the instant could be of any worth to us, if we could be deprived of anything the next instant by whoever was momentarily stronger than ourselves.

As this passage and others in the last of the essays published together as *Utilitarianism* suggest, Mill conceives of security primarily in terms of the reliability of established expectations. Violation of one's legal rights, breach of promise or of contract, the kind of general uncertainty which accompanies both arbitrary despotism and weak government — all these are circumstances in which expectations are subject to unpredictable disappointments which in Mill's view amount to encroachments on the moral right to security. It will be pointed out at once, no doubt, that, if this is all there is to security, then it will be possessed by anyone living in a stable society, whatever its other features. Nor is this false: but two points in qualification need making. First, the number of stable societies in history may well be smaller than those who put this objection imagine. While it is true that a large range of social orders are left in the field when the test of security has been applied, it is not true that the test is so weak as to exclude no social order. Second, it must be pointed out that, in his conception of what security in person and property covered, Mill undoubtedly followed Bentham. He took for granted that, for reasons to do with utility's preconditions, persons should be reliably protected from the physical attacks of their neighbours, from confiscation of property, from arbitrary arrest and so on. If there are good reasons in utility for imposing these more substantive requirements on the test of security (as surely there are) then the range of societies satisfying this more stringent version of the test will be drastically diminished. It may further be observed that while security thus understood imposes a more demanding test on society, it is for that reason a more restrictive standard that is being applied. Once such a conception of security is granted, Mill would be warranted in denying the claims of those — traditionalists or moral conservatives, for example — for whom any form of social change would amount to a violation of their moral right to security.

If there is no radical difficulty in stating the demands of security, the case is admittedly different with regard to the moral right to autonomy. After all, except in a letter to a correspondent,[14] Mill never uses the term 'autonomy' in the context of the argument of *On Liberty*.

It may seem that a conception is being foisted upon Mill in a strained attempt to give his argument a coherence it lacks. Such an impression would be misleading. It is evident that in *On Liberty* Mill argues for liberty — understood here as covering both the absence of moral and legal obligation and the phenomena of force and coercion, which, in their uses by the state, were, of course, connected by Mill with the application of punishment in cases of default in moral or legal obligation — in part by invoking its contribution to another mode of freedom of action. This is the sort of freedom of action, which I have called 'autonomy', which is abridged by what Mill calls 'moral coercion' and which is subverted by the tyrannous public opinion he follows Tocqueville in thinking existed in American democracy. Crucially, unlike security, the moral right to autonomy is possessed, not by all men, but only by those possessing in some minimal degree the capacities of an autonomous agent: it comes into play only at what I have termed the third tier of Mill's hierarchical utilitarianism. As Mill's discussion of individuality in the third chapter of *On Liberty* shows, what matters in autonomy are the powers exercised in framing and implementing successive plans of life. The priority of liberty in Mill's utilitarian account of the moral rights derives in part from its conceptual and empirical connections with autonomy. Autonomy designates the capacities and opportunities involved in self-critical and imaginative choice-making, and the classical liberal freedoms listed in the introductory chapter of *On Liberty* can all be seen as indispensable to the exercise of powers of autonomous thought and action. Because of its links with autonomy, liberty in Mill's doctrine becomes a necessary ingredient of happiness and not just a causally efficacious means to it.

It may be seen that, in Mill's use of the notion, as indeed in the whole tradition flowing from Rousseau and Kant into Humboldt and Tocqueville, and hence into *On Liberty*, autonomy designates a Janus-faced notion. In contrast with conceptions of freedom as self-determination current among the Stoics, for example, autonomy could be abridged both by the interference of others and by intrapersonal failings (such as weakness of will, lack of imagination, etc.). The classical liberal freedoms of association, thought and expression are, for Mill, valuable both as necessary ingredients of autonomy and as instrumentally useful conditions tending to promote autonomy on balance. Thus, though liberty and autonomy are indeed internally related, they are not mutually constitutive; the connection that Mill alleges between them is in some large measure empirically supportable and defeasible.

55

One further point needs to be made about Mill's conception of autonomy. For Mill, and for most of those who work with some such conception of freedom of action, autonomy involves acting on one's current values, projects and life plans. Respecting someone's vital interest in autonomy, then, may sometimes mean allowing him to pursue goals whose achievement damages his lifelong interests in their entirety. This is an unavoidable conclusion, which could be circumvented only by the fraudulent expedient (to which Mill does not resort) of attaching an infinite weight to each man's interest in autonomy. This is an aspect of Mill's argument to which I will address myself more systematically when, in chapter 5, I come to consider his treatment of paternalism. At this stage, I want only to point out that the role that I have attributed to a notion of autonomy in Mill's argument for liberty, becomes readily intelligible in the context of the philosophical psychology that I have ascribed to him. It is, after all, Mill's claim that men are moved to act, not with a view to future pleasure, but by their present associations of actions with pleasure or pain. For Mill, then, while it is true that autonomy desiderates a range of capacities and character traits, which serve as a standard of achievement to which we are to aspire, it is an ideal ingredient of happiness deeply embedded in the nature of human action. Just as security in its weakest form will exist whenever rules are followed, so autonomy exists wherever men act purposively. Though these terms have such universal 'descriptive' connotations, they would also in Mill have had the uses of achievement words, if he had adopted the idiom of 'autonomy' in which to speak of the form of freedom of action which social freedom serves. Indeed, it is Mill's claim that, once the conditions necessary for the possession and exercise of the right to security have been attained, autonomy constitutes a progressively more valuable ingredient of happiness. Of course, stating Mill's claim in this bald form at once suggests difficulties to do with possibilities of conflict between the demands of autonomy and those of security. For, while the two vital interests might not be entirely distinct from one another, neither are they wholly inseparable. At the very least, different policies might affect the interests in autonomy and in security differently, even as they promote or protect both. I leave these difficulties, however, to the last chapter of this study, where I come to appraise the Doctrine of Liberty as a whole.

I have said that Mill's utilitarianism is pluralistic and hierarchical in structure, and I have offered a sketch of how the vital interests in security and in autonomy figure in this hierarchy. I want now to suggest that Mill's theory of vital interests, as given in *On Liberty* and in the last chapter of *Utilitarianism*, gains in plausibility when it is linked to his discussion of the indispensable conditions of social stability in the *Logic*. There we find Mill arguing, in a fashion akin to Hart's arguments about the 'minimum content of natural law' in his *The Concept of Law*,[15] that certain rules or conventions are indispensable to the stability and survival of any society. The use which the term 'harm' is given in *On Liberty* is rule-related inasmuch as the central cases about which Mill is concerned in which harm occurs can typically be represented as involving a breach of those rules which are necessary to social stability and survival. As Mill puts it in *Utilitarianism*, 'a human being is capable of apprehending a community of interest between himself and the human society of which he forms a part, such that any conduct which threatens the security of the society generally, is threatening to his own'.[16] I have already observed that, though not all societies will satisfy the requirements Mill has in mind about security, a large number will do so, few of which come close to resembling a liberal society as Mill conceived of it. How then can Mill narrow the field, so that only those societies remain in which the minimum conditions of natural law are satisfied and in which the claims of liberty are respected? The field is narrowed, in Mill's doctrine, only if the psychological and historical claims embodied in his theory of man are accepted as reasonably founded and probably true. It is these claims that I will examine in the next chapter of this book. Before I can profitably look at the foundation in a view of man of Mill's Doctrine of Liberty, it is necessary to look again at his Principle of Liberty to see if we have freed it of ambiguity and identified correctly its place in his overall doctrine.

2 THE PRINCIPLE OF LIBERTY IN THE DOCTRINE OF LIBERTY

The Principle of Liberty tells us that only the prevention of harm to others can justify limiting liberty. In the first section of this chapter, I have gone to some trouble to specify the conception of harm at work in Mill's principle. I have argued that 'harm to others' is best construed as 'injury to the vital interests of others', where these comprise the interests in autonomy and in security. An area of ambiguity in the

Principle of Liberty I have not discussed, and will not consider here, is engendered by Mill's occasional acknowledgment that not only harm to others, but also a danger of such harm may justify limiting liberty. Introducing calculations of probability into the application of the principle enormously increases its difficulties, but I do not see that the inclusion of endangered or threatened vital interests along with damaged ones is unreasonable or unwarranted in itself. Another area of ambiguity in the principle, and one that is superficially more trouble-some, is that between an interpretation of it as a principle licensing restriction of liberty only to prevent harmful conduct and an interpre-tation as a principle allowing liberty-limitation for the sake of preventing harm. On the first, and more restrictive reading, a man's liberty could rightly be restricted, only if his conduct damaged (or, more leniently, imperilled) the vital interests of others. On the latter reading, a man's liberty might rightly be limited, even if what he was doing affected no one else at all, providing only that such limitation prevented others being harmed. It has been thought by some among Mill's new inter-preters that much turns on whether we read Mill's Principle of Liberty as a harmful conduct principle or else as a general harm-prevention principle, and debate has continued between them as to which is the best supported reading of the principle.

I am inclined to think, with Lyons and against Brown, that Mill understood his principle in harm-prevention rather than in harmful-conduct terms, but I am not much concerned to argue for this inter-pretation.[17] The debate does not go to the heart of the difficulties we have in explicating Mill's Doctrine of Liberty. On either interpretation the principle unequivocally forbids limiting liberty for the sake of general welfare, and the problem of deriving such a principle from utility remains the problem I specified in the first chapter of this book: how could the Principle of Utility support adopting a maxim which disqualifies the promotion of happiness as a reason for action where limiting liberty is at stake? Again, the conflict between the maximisation of a value and its equitable distribution which I specified as another major difficulty for Mill's doctrine crops up on either reading of his principle. It seems to be a greater problem on the more permissive reading of it as a harm-prevention principle, but it remains a major difficulty on the more restrictive reading. Rendering Mill's principle in a permissive form yields the obvious problem that the most cost-effective strategy for minimising harm may not be the most equitable: it reminds us that negative utilitarian strategies about minimising harm (or pain) need be no fairer than positive strategies about maximising happiness or benefit. But the same difficulty is suggested even by the more restrictive reading of the principle. For, even on that reading, a very small harm might seem to justify even a very great loss of liberty, and that loss might be very unevenly and unfairly distributed. Admittedly, the restrictive reading of the Principle of Liberty as a harmful-conduct product has the great advantage that, unless and until harm to others is at issue, all men enjoy the same maximal right to liberty. Inasmuch as it recognises no reason for limiting liberty until there is a question of harm to others, the Principle of Liberty presupposes the classical liberal principle prescribing the greatest possible equal freedom. For, if the principle is accepted, no man may abridge another's freedom unless there is a justification for such abridgment in terms of preventing harm. Once the harm-prevention barrier is crossed, however, restricting liberty is in principle allowable, and we have nothing so far to tell us that we should aim at a fair distribution of restrictions. Even on the restrictive reading, then, a competition between utility and equity reappears, once the barrier erected against ordinary maximisation strategies has been crossed. Finally, I cannot see that the difficulty of finding a utilitarian derivation of Mill's principle is altered whichever interpretation we adopt. All that has been advanced so far about the construal of harm in terms of injury to vital interests might be accepted, and yet the Principle of Liberty itself repudiated. For one might agree that security and autonomy are the weightiest of men's interests, deserving to be ranked over all men's other interests, yet object to even such an apparently weak constraint on the most effective strategy for the protection and promotion of these interests as is constituted by the Principle of Liberty. Whether we interpret it permissively or restrictively, then, the problem with the Principle of Liberty is that it still needs an utilitarian derivation, and, even if that is found, it still seems to need supplementing with an independent principle about distribution. How are these problems to be resolved?

The first link in the chain of connections on which Mill's Doctrine of Liberty depends is that between the protection of vital interests and respect for moral rights. It is the burden of the last chapter of *Utilitarianism* that moral rights are grounded in the vital interests and that justice itself is concerned with the protection of moral rights. It should be noted in passing that Mill is unclear whether the demands of justice are exhausted by the protection of rights, and he fudges the question of whether the obligations of justice may on occasion be defeated by other moral obligations. I consider these difficulties briefly at the end of the next section of this chapter in the context of Mill's view on equity in the doctrine of liberty. Such complications apart, Mill's argument in the last chapter of *Utilitarianism* is that utility demands of us the adoption of a quasi-absolute principle having to do with respect for moral rights. In *Utilitarianism* the moral right identified and most centrally acknowledged is that grounded in the interest in security, whereas in *On Liberty* it is the vital interests in autonomy that is central. In both texts, however, it is clear that Mill's argument is that utility itself demands the adoption of a weighty (but not infinitely weighty) side-constraint principle about the protection of moral rights.

That this side-constraint principle *is* the Principle of Liberty follows only if we are prepared to allow credibility to the theory of vital interests. Equally, the Principle of Liberty can be grounded in the theory of the vital interests only if we are ready to allow that direct strategies for promoting welfare are self-defeating. Here Mill seems to want to distinguish, as does A. K. Sen,[18] between principles which impose informational constraints on the considerations we are allowed to take into account in practical deliberation and other, more basic principles. Taking *On Liberty* and *Utilitarianism* together, his argument seems to be that we will not best protect and promote the vital interests if we try to move directly to that end. We find our best chance in the strategy embodied in the Principle of Liberty — the strategy of curtailing liberty only when the vital interests of others are at risk. But how does this Principle of Liberty figure in the Doctrine of Liberty as a whole? Though I have not gone so far as to claim that the Principle of Liberty presupposes the rest of Mill's theory of justice, I want to argue that the meaning of harm-prevention is given in the discussion of the vital interests and of the moral rights grounded in their protection which Mill undertakes in the last chapter of *Utilitarianism*. If this linkage in Mill's writings is acknowledged to be intelligible and plausible, we can begin to see how Mill may have viewed the restriction of utilitarian policy to harm-prevention, and the narrowing of harm-prevention to injury to the vital interests as strategies defensible in utilitarian terms. The chief interest of Mill's indirect utilitarianism, in fact, is that it issues in a conception of justice defended precisely in these terms.

Before I try to fill out more systematically the connection of the Principle of Liberty with Mill's theory of justice, it is worth confronting a common objection to the moral soundness of Mill's theory which I think can easily be shown to rest on a simple understanding. This is the objection, clearly and forcefully put by Brown, that 'we have duties to help other people which go beyond the avoidance of harming them; that the performance of such duties can legitimately be exacted from us, very commonly in our roles as citizens and taxpayers; and that such exactions are not permitted by Mill's main principle'.[19] Brown's objection is made even by those who do not accept his reading of the Principle of Liberty in harmful-conduct terms; for do we not have moral duties that go beyond merely preventing harm and extend actually to assisting or benefiting people? Now I am not here considering cases, treated by Mill himself and not the principal object of his critics' attacks, where an omission may be seen as itself harmful. Beyond such cases of emergency or Good Samaritanism, it may well be held desirable, and even perhaps as morally obligatory, that we actually assist people to make the best of their lives. Does not the Principle of Liberty stand in the way of such helping in all those cases where it does not take the form of voluntary charity? Does not the Principle of Liberty condemn all effort on the part of state or governmental agencies to help or benefit people in cases where harm-prevention is not at issue?

It is fascinating in this connection to note Mill's observation in the last chapter of *On Liberty* that he has[20]

> reserved for the last place a large class of questions respecting to limits of government interference which, though closely connected with the subject of this Essay, do not, in strictness, belong to it. There are cases in which the reasons against interference do not turn upon the principle of liberty; the question is not about restraining the actions of individuals, but about helping them; it is asked whether the government should do, or cause to be done, something for their benefit, instead of leaving it to be done by themselves, individually or in voluntary combination.

The crucial impact of this passage is that reasons against interference are not given by the Principle of Liberty but by other, broader considerations of general expediency. As a rule, Mill goes on to argue, people are best left to help themselves without state or governmental assistance, which typically has a stultifying and paralysing effect on initiative and energy. These considerations of expediency do not, however, support a quasi-absolute prohibition on positive state action to benefit or help and are never represented in *On Liberty* as doing so. The principle of government non-interference in social life, mentioned by Mill in *On Liberty* and defended by him at length in the relevant portions of his *Principles of Political Economy*, is characterised by Mill himself as a conclusion of expediency, a fallible rule of thumb whose application is a matter of time, place and circumstance. In short, it carries none of that stringency and weight borne by the Principle of Liberty. The reason is clear enough if we recall Mill's distinction (made in *Principles of Political Economy*) between authoritative and non-authoritative uses of governmental authority:[21]

> We must set out by distinguishing between two kinds of intervention by the government, which, though they may relate to the same subject, differ widely in their nature and effects, and require, for their justification, motives of a very different degree of urgency. The intervention may extend to controlling the free agency of individuals. Government may interdict all persons from doing certain things; or from doing them without its authorization; or may prescribe to them certain things to be done, or a certain manner of doing things which it is left optional with them to do or abstain from. This is the *authoritative* interference by government. There is another kind which is not authoritative: when a government, instead of issuing a command and enforcing it by penalties, adopts the course so seldom reverted to by governments, and of which such important use might be made, that of giving advice or promulgating information; or when, leaving individuals free to use their own means of pursuing any object of general interest, the government, not meddling with them, but not trusting the object solely to their care, establishes, side by side with their arrangements, an agency of its own for a like purpose . . .
>
> It is evident, even at first sight, that the authoritative form of government interference has a much more limited sphere of legitimate action than the other. It requires a much stronger necessity to justify it in any case; while there are large departments of human life from which it must be unreservedly and imperiously excluded.

Authoritative governmental agency, then, is essentially prohibitive or coercive and encompasses the restriction of liberty, whereas non-authoritative action involves no coercion or limitation of liberty beyond that which is necessary for the raising of general state revenues. My submission here is that the Principle of Liberty is proposed by Mill for the control only of what he had earlier designated 'authoritative' governmental action and has nothing to say about government actions, whether for the benefit of others or merely to prevent harm to them, when such action involves no infringement of liberty beyond that already entailed in the tax-raising power. There is, then, no inconsistency in Mill's identifying in his *Principles of Political Economy* a large range of desirable state activities having nothing to do with harm-prevention and later proposing his Principle of Liberty. For the latter concerns only the curtailment of liberty and is not breached by state activity of any sort, providing it occurs outside the authoritative sphere.

3 UTILITY, JUSTICE AND THE TERMS OF SOCIAL CO-OPERATION IN THE DOCTRINE OF LIBERTY

At the very start of this inquiry, I confronted a fundamental objection to any utilitarian theory of moral rights. How can a strong commitment to individual moral rights coexist with an affirmation of the overriding claims of general welfare? After all, moral rights are commonly taken as trumping the claims of general welfare − as, in other words, framing moral constraints on the pursuit of utility. Mill himself alludes to the question in the last chapter of *Utilitarianism*: 'To have a right, then, is, I conceive, to have something which society ought to defend me in the possession of. If the objector goes on to ask, why it ought? I can give him no other reason than general utility.'[22] How is this fundamental challenge to be countered?

It can be countered, if Mill is right in supposing that direct appeal to utility has a self-defeating effect, and if his argument is cogent, which supports the claim that this self-defeating effect provides a utilitarian warrant for adopting a side-constraint principle instead of the utility principle as the dominant principle about limitation of liberty in a civilised society. That the side-constraint principle in question *is* the liberty principle can be argued for, only if we are prepared to allow credibility to Mill's conception of human nature.

As I have remarked already, it is clear that, if the liberty principle is construed as forbidding restriction of liberty except when damage to vital interests (and so violation of moral rights) is threatened, then, by the same token, liberty-limiting intervention to benefit some at the expense of others is forbidden. Nothing is added to the liberty principle by the requirement that moral rights to security and autonomy be distributed equally, since the liberty principle (unlike that of utility) actually presupposes such a requirement. If the liberty principle is (as I have earlier contended) to be construed in this way as a side-constraint principle forbidding trade-offs between the vital interests and other human interests, how can it be shown to flow from a utility principle whose maximising implications I have not contested? Mill's own view of this question should not be in doubt. In *Thornton on Labour and Its Claims*[23] he asserts:

> Mr. Thornton seems to admit the general happiness as the criterion of social virtue but not of positive duty — not of justice and injustice in the strict sense: and he imagines that it is in making a distinction between these two ideas that his doctrine differs from that of utilitarian moralists. But this is not the case. Utilitarian morality fully recognises the distinction between the province of positive duty and that of virtue, but maintains that the standard and rule of both is the general interest. From the utilitarian point of view, the distinction then is the following: — There are many acts, and a still greater number of forbearances, the perpetual practice of which by all is so necessary to the general well-being, that people must be held to it compulsively, either by law, or by social pressure. These acts and forbearances constitute duty. Outside these bounds there is the innumerable variety of modes in which the acts of human beings are either a cause, or a hindrance, of good to their fellow-creatures, but to which it is, on the whole, for the general interest that they should be left free; being merely encouraged, by praise and honour, to the performance of such beneficial actions as are not sufficiently stimulated by benefits flowing from them to the agent himself. This larger sphere is that of Merit or Virtue.

Again, in a passage in *August Comte and Positivism*,[24] part of which I have already quoted, Mill says:

> It is incumbent on every one to restrain the pursuit of his personal objects within the limits consistent with the essential interests of others. What these limits are, it is the province of ethical science to determine; and to keep all individuals within them, is the proper office of punishment and of moral blame .... The proper office of those sanctions is to enforce upon every one, the conduct necessary to give all other persons their fair chance: conduct which

chiefly consists in not doing them harm, and not impeding them in anything which without harming others does good to themselves.

Further, in his review of George Cornewall Lewis's book, *The Use and Abuse of Political Terms*, Mill observes:[25]

Whatever obligation any man would lie under in a state of nature, not to inflict evil upon another for the sake of good to himself, the same obligation lies upon society towards every one of its members. If he injure or molest any one of his fellow citizens, the consequences of whatever they may be obliged to do in self-defence, must fall upon himself; but otherwise the government fails in its duty, if on any plea of doing good to the community in the aggregate, it reduces him to such a state, that he is on the whole a loser by living in a state of government, and would have been better off if it did not exist. This is the truth which was dimly shadowed forth, in howsoever rude and unskilful a manner, in the theories of the social compact and of the rights of man.

These passages are liable to a variety of interpretations, but a number of claims show through clearly enough. Mill seems to regard practical moral principles such as his Principle of Liberty as useful in part as framing the terms of social co-operation. The Principle of Utility itself is seen as unfitted for the role of a public and practical principle, not only because of its axiological character, but because it could impose upon members of society demands (in terms of a sacrifice of their vital interests) which they could not help regarding as unreasonable and which would be bound to disturb the stability of the social union. For Mill, no less than for Rawls, a principle setting the terms of social co-operation is disqualified if, because of certain general facts of human nature, it is incapable of generating social stability and a sense of loyalty to public institutions. Mill's conjecture is that, whereas Utility is thus disqualified, the Principle of Liberty passes this test (and can be shown to be felicific in many other respects). The Principle of Liberty is recommended by Mill, accordingly, as a sort of *maximising constraint* on policy. Though he could not have expressed it in such terms, the intuition underlying Mill's statements is that a higher maximum of utility is attainable in a world where policy is bounded by the constraint of the Principle of Liberty than could be attained by the direct and unconstrained pursuit of utility. The idea of such a maximising constraint may sound difficult or paradoxical, but it is not incoherent and it gains in credibility if it is allowed that the direct pursuit of happiness is collectively self-defeating.

It is important to be clear what is not claimed in these and similar passages. Mill does not say that coercion is only ever justified if it aims to defeat coercion. He does not espouse here a policy governed by the principle of limiting liberty only for the sake of liberty; he recognises implicitly, as he acknowledges explicitly in *On Liberty*, that individual liberty may rightly be limited for the sake of the prevention of harm. Again, though he repudiates policies as a result of which a man may be worse off on balance than he would be in an anarchical state of nature, and does so even where they might reasonably be thought likely to yield maximum aggregate welfare, Mill does not hold that any man's moral rights are inviolable. Robert Nozick wavers at the point where refusing to violate a moral right would bring about moral catastrophe,[26] and Rawls's doctrine explicitly allows for infringements of liberty under the general conception of justice.[27] Mill's argument, rather, is that principles such as his Principle of Liberty are public and practical principles for the appraisal of policies adopted as such by men aware that their continuing partiality to their own interests subverts any direct appeal to Utility as a principle capable of sustaining a stable social union. In this Mill's doctrine resembles the species of co-operative utilitarianism identified and defended by Regan as the only form of consequentialism which recognises the equality and interdependence of moral persons as they act to produce consequences.[28] Mill's Doctrine of Liberty has a Kantian and a Rawlsian aspect as well in that the terms of social co-operation it requires include the protection of the vital interests, conceived of as minimal conditions of stable social union, but not the positive promotion of social welfare by means which involved the limitation of liberty. The Doctrine of Liberty has this Kantian and Rawlsian aspect inasmuch as the Principle of Liberty which it comprehends allows invasion of liberty only where such invasion facilitates the protection of moral rights — in the restrictive version of the principle, only where there has been a departure from non-aggression. Even if it licenses a utilitarianism of rights,[29] Mill's doctrine forbids (except in extremity) the trading off of rights for other advantages.

We are still left with the question whether the Doctrine of Liberty needs and has room for a Principle of Equity — a principle distinct from and independent of the Principle of Liberty. It is to some such principle, presumably, that Mill alludes when he tells us that each man's share of 'the labours and sacrifices incurred for defending the society or its members' should be determined on 'some equitable principle'.[30] It seems plain enough that the Doctrine of Liberty will have incomplete action-guiding force if it lacks such a principle, but Mill nowhere gives us any guidance as to how a Principle of Equity is to be framed. Mill needs a maxim guiding us as to how much liberty may be traded away for how much harm-prevention. It would be unfair to say that the Doctrine of Liberty gives no guidance at all in this area. It forbids invasion of vital interests, including the interest in autonomy, save to forestall catastrophe, and so protects a universal minimum of welfare in all normal circumstances. Again, in protecting the vital interests in autonomy, the Principle of Liberty itself safeguards a measure of equality inasmuch as autonomy precludes relationships of domination. These are not very determinate guides, it is true, but it may be that Mill thought his principle of equity could not in fact be stated very precisely. However that may be, it is clear that he is committed to treating such a principle of equity as another derivation of utility. If I am correct in treating the Principle of Liberty as a major part of Mill's substantive theory of justice, then the undefined Principle of Equity would figure in that theory as supplementing the Principle of Liberty and completing the Doctrine of Liberty.

The Doctrine of Liberty seems, then, to comprehend maxims other than the Principles of Utility and of Liberty but, like the latter, any such additional principle is defended as a derivation of Utility itself. Apart from the (unstated) maxim about fairness I have mentioned, there is much evidence to suggest that Mill regards the harm-prevention allowed by the liberty principle as framing the boundaries of moral obligation. Thus we have the Principle of Liberty figuring as a precept of justice, protecting essential interests (which alone ground moral rights) save where harm to others is at stake, and we have a negative-utilitarian account of moral obligation as concerned solely with harm-prevention. Where, as with 'non-authoritative' interference, government action is taken to assist valuable activity and ventures at no cost in liberty, and these ventures are not justifiable on harm-prevention grounds, Mill is committed to regarding such state activity as analogous to voluntary private charity, in other words, as a wholly discretionary exercise of beneficence not demanded by a definite moral obligation.

There is some unclarity in Mill, not only (as I have already observed) on the question of whether moral assessment always concerns only questions of moral obligation, but also on the question of whether the requirements of justice are coextensive with the protection of moral rights. At times, Mill seems almost to wish to run together morality with moral obligation, moral obligation with the requirements of justice and justice itself with the protection of rights, but this cannot in consistency represent his considered view. For, apart from the fact that occasionally he speaks of supererogatory acts as morally praiseworthy, Mill famously distinguishes in *Utilitarianism* between 'perfect' and 'imperfect' obligations[31] and classifies Good Samaritanism as involving moral obligation but not of the 'perfect' sort emanating from justice. Again, Mill seems to want to treat the Principle of Equity, which I have sought to clarify above, as framing a demand of justice, but it is not plausibly interpreted as concerned with rights-protection since breach of it will not typically cause damage to the vital interests of assignable individuals (even where it involves injury to harm-preventing public institutions or practices).[32] Whereas what Mill has to say on these questions is not always clear, consistent and persuasive, it is not at all obvious that these lapses in his doctrine constitute fatal flaws in it. Mill's doctrine is in the combination of claims that, whereas only harm to vital interests can justify restricting liberty, the general interest dictates selection of those harm-prevention policies that are least costly in terms of damage to vital interests. My claim is that the first of these claims is intelligibly linked with the account of justice given in utilitarian terms in the last chapter of *Utilitarianism*, but the second is a direct deduction from the demands of expediency taken in the context of the general facts of human social life. The Doctrine of Liberty rests in part on Mill's theory of justice, then, but it is not exhausted by it.

The limitation of liberty-limiting policy to harm-prevention and the restriction of harm-prevention to policies not involving damage to essential interests are each defended in Mill as utilitarian strategies. The Principle of Liberty, its presuppositions and its implications, thus frame the terms of social cooperation and are regarded as strategic principles defensible in utilitarian terms. Mill's Doctrine of Liberty invokes his overall utilitarian theory of moral rights, which rests on a conjecture about which practical maxims ought to be adopted if utility is to be promoted. Like the rest of his doctrine, it trades on his view of man, without which it lacks credibility. One objection to Mill's enterprise, indeed, is that his view of man is tailor-made to fit his partisan ideals, so that a genuinely supportive role cannot be played in his theory by a conception of human nature. As against this, I wish to argue in the next chapter that Mill advances independently criticisable psychological and historical claims about human nature and development which go some distance towards sustaining his theory.

IV

MILL'S CONCEPTION OF HAPPINESS AND THE THEORY OF INDIVIDUALITY

1 INDIVIDUALITY, HAPPINESS AND THE HIGHER PLEASURES

Mill's Doctrine of Liberty is supported by a view of human happiness which in turn depends on his conception of human nature. Evident in both *On Liberty* and *Utilitarianism* is Mill's belief that the forms of happiness which are most distinctively human are unachievable except against a background of autonomy and security. Human happiness in its fullest expression presupposes a social order in which the vital interests are reliably protected and in which, also, a certain level of cultural and moral development has been generally achieved. So much, I hope, has been argued persuasively in the previous chapters of this book. I want now to argue that there is an important and largely neglected link between the theory of the higher pleasures in *Utilitarianism* and the account of individuality given in the third chapter of *On Liberty*. The link is found in the idea of autonomous choice which is a necessary ingredient of any higher pleasure and of any form of life or activity expressive of individuality. I want to claim, in fact, that the doctrine of the higher pleasures is not only not the absurdity it has often been represented as, but also a component of the Doctrine of Liberty. According to Mill's theory of qualitative hedonism, the higher pleasures are found in forms of life and activity whose content is distinctive and peculiar in each case, but which necessarily involve the exercise of generically human power of autonomous thought and action. It is these forms of life, distinctively human but peculiar in each case, that Mill sees as expressing individuality and as being open to all only in a society in which the Principle of Liberty is respected and enforced.

Having sketched these links in the Doctrine of Liberty, we are left with a number of puzzles. We need to know how autonomous choice connects in Mill's theory with the development of individuality and the achievement of the higher pleasures, and only then can we command a view of the ways in which the theory of the higher pleasures supports the Doctrine of Liberty. Our task is not an easy one for a number of reasons. Despite his inclination to self-criticism, Mill was rarely explicit about the basic notions deployed in his arguments, and it is rare to come across any formal definition of the terms he employs. Further, as I have noted already, 'autonomy' is not a term he employs himself, and I need to support my claim that a conception of autonomous choice is, in fact, central to the argument of *On Liberty*. It is unavoidable that I will use terms and distinctions that would have seemed foreign to Mill, and inevitable that my interpretation must be in the nature of a frankly conjectural reconstruction rather than a literal rendition of Mill's argument. Nevertheless, though it will involve imposing on Mill's writings a terminology that would be unfamiliar to him, I shall claim that it reflects and expresses Mill's underlying commitments and concerns better than any other we have currently at our disposal. The test of its efficacy can only be in whether it yields a plausible and coherent view of Mill's argument. How, then, does Mill's conception of happiness support the Doctrine of Liberty?

We can begin to sort this out if we acknowledge the abstractness and complexity of Mill's conception of happiness. For all his references to pleasure and the absence of pain, Mill never endorsed the primitive view that pleasure is a sort of sensation that accompanies our actions. Mill's departures from Benthamite utilitarianism were in part motivated by an awareness of the inadequacies of the moral psychology of classical utilitarianism. While he continues to adhere to a belief in the uniformity of human nature (in that he never abandons the belief that the way to render human actions intelligible and to explain them is to subsume them under some law-like principles), he breaks with the Enlightenment belief in its constancy. Though he affirms that a science of ethology (the study of the laws of formation of character) will one day ascertain the laws of mind, he goes further than Hume, who acknowledged that variable customs and institutions alter men's motives, in ascribing to human nature a potentiality for unpredictable mutation and for self-transformation. His conception of human nature

and his view of happiness accordingly have an ineradicable developmental and historical dimension. His conception of happiness has this
historical dimension in that Mill affirms that certain general cultural
achievements are indispensable before the fullest happiness becomes
achievable by many men. It has a developmental aspect, also, inasmuch
as Mill was committed to a view of moral development and personal
growth as having several distinct phases. These matters are sketchily
treated in Mill, but it is not fanciful to discern such conceptions in his
writings. How then does Mill suggest we conceive of human happiness?

Mill's conception of happiness is hierarchical and pluralistic in that
it decomposes happiness into the projects, attachments and ideals expressed in an indefinitely large set of happy human lives. If we treat
Mill's distinction between the higher and lower pleasures as being
between different kinds of activity or forms of life rather than between
states of mind, we can see that, though he is far from supposing that
the higher pleasures will be the same for all men, he does think they
have the common feature of being available only to men who have
developed their distinctively human capacity for autonomous thought
and action. Mill's view is not, indeed, that highly autonomous men are
bound to be happy, but rather that autonomous thought and action is
a necessary feature of the life of a man who enjoys the higher pleasures.
What more is involved in autonomy, however, than choice-making and
an imaginative awareness of alternative forms of life-activity?

Before I attempt to answer that difficult question, it may be worth
looking in greater detail at the connections I have postulated between
the argument of *On Liberty* and the much-abused doctrine of the
higher pleasures in *Utilitarianism*. First, what is the relation between
the notion of autonomous choice (which, as I shall argue, is central
to the idea of a free man as it is elaborated in *On Liberty*) and the
higher pleasures of *Utilitarianism*? Is the connection between autonomous choice and the higher pleasures criterial, or is it merely evidential?
If what a man chooses autonomously is the criterion for what is a
higher pleasure for him, then he cannot be mistaken as to what are his
higher pleasures so long as his choices are autonomous, and, if the
pattern of his autonomous choices changes, then so must the content
of his higher pleasures. If, on the other hand, the connection between
the higher pleasures and autonomous choices is that the latter afford
evidence for the content of the former, we need some guidance as to
the criteria for the higher pleasures.

I want to argue that this distinction between a criterial and an

72

evidential view of the relations between autonomy and the higher pleasures fails to capture the spirit of Mill's view of the matter. There can be no doubt that Mill does take choice-making to be itself a necessary ingredient of happiness and of any higher pleasure: it is a necessary condition of a pleasure being a higher pleasure that it consist in activities that have been chosen after experience of an appropriate range of alternatives. But the sufficient condition of a pleasure's being a higher pleasure is that it express the individual nature of the man whose pleasure it is, and this, for the man himself as for others, is a matter of discovery and not of choice. Mill's position here is a complex one. On the one hand, like Aristotle, he affirmed that men were the makers of their own characters. On the other hand, there is no doubt that Mill held to the Romantic belief that each has a quiddity or essence which awaits his discovery and which, if he is lucky, he may express in any one of a small number of styles of life. Mill seems, in his complex view, to be treating choice-making as itself partially constitutive of a happy human life and as instrumental to it. How are these different accounts of the role of autonomous choice-making in human happiness brought together in Mill's theory of individuality?

Another question suggests itself. Inasmuch as Mill put autonomous choice at the heart of the higher pleasures and of those forms of individuality or self-development in which the higher pleasures are found, and inasmuch as he denied that there can be a duty to develop oneself, it is clear that the higher pleasures are to be appraised by aesthetic and prudential rather than by moral standards. Moral life may contain higher pleasures, no doubt, but the place of morality is to protect and permit the higher pleasures, not to demand them. Part of the rationale of adopting the Principle of Liberty is that an open space in which the higher pleasures may flourish is thereby guaranteed. But what if men do not converge on the higher pleasures: suppose, after due thought and experiment, they come to prefer forms of life and activity in which autonomous choice is an insignificant ingredient — what then? Does the Doctrine of Liberty presuppose that the condition of freedom is irreversible and the human preference for the higher pleasures unshakeable?

2 AUTONOMY, AUTHENTICITY AND CHOICE-MAKING

In order to answer these questions, we need to look more closely at what is comprehended in the notion of autonomy. We may begin our examination by recalling the conception of freedom as self-determination, expressed by the Stoic philosophers. On this view, a man may be said to act freely, if and only if he has engaged in rational deliberation on the alternatives open to him. This conception of freedom as rational self-direction could properly be used of a slave or an agent acting under coercion, providing only that he succeeds in acting in accordance with his own rational policies. The conception of freedom as rational self-direction serves to distinguish the freedom of action of the agent who, though he may act under coercion, yet exhibits powers of rational reflection and possesses strength of will, from the freedom of the agent who, possessing neither strength of will nor a rational life-plan, may none the less be said to be free to act in respect of an action in so far as his doing of that action is not prevented by the forcible or coercive intervention of another – who (in other words) possesses negative freedom in respect of that action.[1] My first point, then, is that an agent may possess this negative freedom and yet lack the freedom of rational self-direction, and vice versa.

A stronger form of freedom to act is denoted by the term 'autarchy'. What is understood by an agent's being autarchic? In its uses in recent discussions,[2] discourse concerning autarchic agency denotes the freedom of action of an agent who, while enjoying (over a wide range of actions) that negative freedom which covers the absence both of force and of coercion, also exercises unimpaired all the normal capacities and powers of a rational chooser by reference to which freedom as rational self-direction is defined. Another form of freedom may now be distinguished – that of the autonomous man. How may we tell an agency which is autarchic from that which is autonomous? Clearly, an autonomous agent will possess all the defining features of an autarchic agent: but, in addition to exercising capacities for rational reflection and strength of will in the objective choice-conditions which are not distorted by the presence of force or coercion, an autonomous agent must also have distanced himself in some measure from the conventions of his social environment and from the influence of the persons surrounding him. His actions express principles and policies which he has himself ratified by a process of critical reflection.

Plainly, even more straightforwardly than is the case with autarchy, autonomous agency must be regarded as something which must be achieved (and which can never be achieved completely) rather than as a natural human endowment or original inheritance.

The distinction between autarchic status and the status of an

74

autonomous agent may become clearer if we look at some of the ways in which an agent may be disqualified from autonomy but not from autarchy. We may begin by noting that an agent falls short of being autarchic if his behaviour is recognisably compulsive, based on delusive ideas which he cannot evaluate critically, and which incapacitate him from making rational choices between real-world options. An agent may fail to be autarchic, also, in so far as his behaviour is governed by someone else by whom he may be dominated, mesmerised or over-awed: of such an agent we may say that he is heterarchic, one governed, not by himself, but by another. We may wish to say of a heterarchic agent that his normal functioning as a chooser has been impaired by the intervention of another, so that his decisions are his own only in a Pickwickian sense − in reality they are the decisions of another. Since the heterarchic agent's conduct is governed, not by any will of his own, but by the will of another, it is plain enough that his freedom of action has been effectively curtailed; but it remains important to distinguish clearly between this kind of loss of freedom and that which occurs whenever an agent acts under coercion. Whenever coercion occurs, one will is subordinated to another: the coerced agent is no longer an independent actor, since his will has been overborne by the will of the coercer. An agent remains self-determining (though not autarchic) even when he acts under coercion: for, in that any instance of coercion involves a conflict of wills, any claim that a man has been coerced pre-supposes that the coerced agent retains a will of his own, which is not true of the strictly heterarchical agent. (I do not deny that the long-run effect, and in some cases the aim, of coercion may be to destroy or at least impair the capacities involved in being a self-determining agent. This possibility creates complications I cannot go into here, except to say that where coercion does destroy the capacities for self-determination it is plausible to think that the unfreedom of coercion has been re-placed by another − and worse − form of unfreedom.) A coerced agent, then, cannot be other than an agent capable of rational self-direction and so of self-determination.

The point that only those capable of rational self-direction can be said to suffer coercion may be brought out again by considering cases in which an agent may be disqualified from autarchy without being heterarchic: such are the cases of 'anomic' or 'wanton' individuals, for example, as Frankfurt[3] has termed them. Individuals who fall into this class satisfy the conditions of human agency: they are individuals whose desires are not ordered into any stable hierarchy, and who lack any standards by appeal to which they may judge and perhaps repress the inclinations of the moment. An anomic or wanton individual, then, is one who possesses no ideal image of himself by reference to which he may assess his own performances. Frankfurt has stated[4] that the defining feature of a wanton is that he does not care about his will, and so has none of the second-order desires and volitions the possession of which serves to distinguish persons from animals and from some human beings: the class of wantons includes all (or, more cautiously, almost all) non-human animals, all human infants and some adult human beings. Since an anomic individual lacks a will of his own of the kind we ordinarily attribute to persons, there can be no implication of any ascription of anomic status that his will has been overborne by that of another (as in cases of coercion), or that the will of another has been substituted for it (as in cases of heterarchy). Manifestly, in so far as coercion always involves a conflict of will, it is no more possible to coerce a wanton than to coerce an animal or an infant (though all three may be subject to force). Only a very restricted conception of negative freedom as the absence of force, then, is applicable to the class of wantons: the wanton cannot be said to have that kind of freedom (of which self-determination, autarchy and autonomy are instances) the possession of which would warrant ascribing to him responsibility for his actions and the absence of which in his case acts as a permanent excusing condition.

I have observed that one of the most important ways in which an agent may be disqualified from autarchy is by being heterarchic. It is evident, also, that an agent who is not heterarchic may yet be heteronomous. For a man may have all the attributes of a rational chooser (including a will of his own) and yet be wholly under the sway of custom, habit or the expectations of his peer group. In David Riesman's useful terminology,[5] he may be 'other-directed' — he may act unreflectively on standards and principles which he has taken over from his social and cultural environment without ever subjecting them to a critical evaluation. Such an agent, though not properly speaking heterarchic, is yet heteronomous in that his conduct is governed by a law (nomos) which he has taken over from others, without due thought, and which is not his own in the required sense. One of the crucial differences between autarchy and autonomy may be located in the fact that an autonomous agent is one who, in Rousseau's expression, acts in obedience to a law he has prescribed for himself. In Frankfurt's idiom,[6] an autonomous agent is one who has a will of his own, who

who has subjected his volitions to a sustained critical evaluation, who has the opportunity to translate his will into action, and whose will is free. It is important to note that the last two of these four conditions are not equivalent, but distinct. For the question of whether a person's will is free is not the question of whether he is in a position to translate his first order desires into actions; the latter question is the question of whether an agent is free to act as he wants to act; it is the question of whether coercive interferences (for example) prevent him from acting as he wants to act. By contrast, freedom of will means here rather that an agent is free to want that which he wants to want. To act freely in the formal sense means to act as an autarchic agent; while, if an agent enjoys both the freedom of action of an autarchic agent, and also freedom of will, then he may qualify as an autonomous agent proper. The dual aspect of autonomous agency, which I have expressed by saying that an autonomous agent acts freely and has freedom of will is happily captured by Joel Feinberg, when he says: 'I am autonomous if I rule me, and no-one else rules I.'[7]

It is evident that the four conceptions of freedom which I have tried to elucidate — negative freedom, rational self-direction, autarchy and autonomy — have been characterised in such a fashion that autonomy embraces the previous three, inasmuch as anyone who may be said to enjoy the freedom of autonomy will possess these other modes of freedom too. A society of autonomous agents, then, would be a society whose members enjoyed legal immunity in the exercise of certain important powers and of whom it was also true that they had developed these capacities and abilities up to at least a minimum level. The Janus-faced aspect of the concept of autonomy is disclosed in the fact that every application of it must make reference at once to a range of legal liberties and to a span of personal powers to act in ways characteristic of those of whom autonomous agency is predicated. It is worth emphasising that autonomy is abridged not only when actions are prevented by some external obstruction such as forcible restraint or the threat of legal punishment, but, more fundamentally, when the pressure of public opinion is such that certain options are not even conceivable, or, if conceivable, not treated as genuine candidates for viable forms of life. Mill argues for liberty, not because he believes that, once liberty is protected, there will be a society of free men; rather, he seeks to promote a society of free or autonomous men, and argues that this is impossible of achievement if liberty is curtailed beyond the domain circumscribed by his principle.

The reader may reasonably doubt if the apparatus of terms and distinctions I have sketched has any basis in Mill's writings but, though the reservation is not unreasonable in that these distinctions are not in any sense derived from Mill's work, it is groundless if it implies that nothing in Mill's writings corresponds to them. Mill's exclusion of children, the mentally unbalanced and backward peoples from the sphere of application of the Principle of Liberty suggests strongly that he regarded the autarchic status as a necessary condition of the application of the principle. What evidence is there, though, of Mill's holding to an ideal of personal autonomy? Much the clearest evidence occurs in the famous third chapter of *On Liberty*. Consider the following passage:[8]

> The human faculties of perception, judgement, discriminative feeling, mental activity, and even moral preference, are exercised only in making a choice. He who does anything because it is the custom makes no choice . . . The mental and moral, like the muscular powers, are improved only by being used.

Again:[9]

> A person whose desires and impulses are his own — are the expression of his own nature, as it has been developed and modified by his own culture — is said to have a character. One whose desires and impulses are not his own, has no character, no more than a steam-engine has a character.

We find here unmistakable traces of a Kantian conception of autonomy, absorbed by Mill (in a neo-Romantic variant) from Humboldt. Despite the absence in his writings of any explicit use of the jargon of autonomy and authenticity, I think we are on firm ground if we include an ideal of personal autonomy among Mill's most fundamental commitments. A man failed to be a free man in Mill's view, if he was subject to force or coercion in the self-regarding area, or if the pressure of public opinion were brought to bear in that area. Human beings failed to be autonomous if — as was the case of women in traditional marriage arrangements, according to Mill — they lacked the opportunity to develop wills of their own and to act on them. In this latter case, which Mill examines at length in *The Subjection of Women*, it is the condition of heterarchy that thwarts autonomy. The more widespread condition of heteronomy which Mill attacks in *On Liberty* is that in which human beings constantly defer to the pressures of social convention and public opinion, submitting their own tastes (if they have any tastes of their own) to the anonymous arbitration of the mass. There is no doubt that Mill saw much of the importance of the Principle of Liberty in its disfavouring this latter sort of heteronomy (even if the adoption of the principle by society could not itself positively promote autonomy). But, further, there can be no doubt either that Mill saw the striving for autonomy as a permanent part, though an easily thwarted part, of the human striving for happiness. It is fair to say, indeed, that Mill would have represented this ideal as an adaptation of the Benthamite conception of happiness to the realities of human psychology. I will return to this point in the last section of this chapter.

We may now return to our original question: What more is involved in being autonomous than making choices based upon an imaginative appreciation of alternative forms of life? We come now to a fundamental aspect of Mill's theory of individuality, namely his claim that a man who attains or displays individuality will have desires and projects of his own — he will, in the idiom I have adopted, exhibit authenticity. A crucial question, now, is how authenticity is related to autonomy. On some accounts, such as Ladenson's, authenticity is collapsible into autonomy. As Ladenson puts it, 'For Mill . . . the cultivation of individuality is the development of reason.'[10] Though that claim captures an aspect of Mill's theory of individuality, it neglects an aspect, too. For Mill, as I have pointed out, a man displays individuality only if his desires and projects are his own. No doubt, reason — self-criticism, careful thought and so on — will typically be an indispensable means for any agent to determine what are his projects and desires; but the point is that for Mill, this is partly a matter of discovery. On Mill's account, autonomy and authenticity are not equivalent, since a man could display autonomy in a very high measure, and yet (in virtue of false beliefs, perhaps) be mistaken as to where his unique endowments and potentialities lie. Part of the rationale for encouraging experiments in living, after all, is that they are aids in attaining self-knowledge (which may, in turn, be useful to others). If there were not a cognitive dimension to judgments about which desires and projects are my own, if such judgments were in the end in the nature of sheer groundless commitments, the argument for liberty would no longer have the instrumental aspect which it must retain if it is to be in any relevant respect a utilitarian argument. It would be an argument appealing primarily or simply to the value of choice; and, to that extent, a less complex, less persuasive and less interesting argument than Mill's.

It is not hard to find in the text of *On Liberty* itself passages lending support to the interpretation I have advanced. Mill asserts:[11]

> Human nature is not a machine to be built after a model, and set to
> do exactly the work prescribed for it, but a tree, which requires to
> grow and develop itself on all sides, according to the tendency of the
> inward forces which make it a living thing.

Here we have a form of expression suggesting, in Aristotelian fashion,
that there is a natural tendency in men to self-realisation which social
arrangements may nurture or thwart. Admittedly, Mill's conviction of
the oppressive force of custom and tradition led him to take a deeply
pessimistic view of the capacity of the great majority of men to assert
their inborn tendencies against established traditions and conventions.
Still, the teleological language which Mill uses, and the whole context
of his discussion, suggest the thesis that each man has a unique range
of potentialities, expressible in a relatively small range of possible lives,
and that the actualisation of these potentialities is indispensable for any
man's greatest well-being. This thesis is one of the hinges on which the
argument of *On Liberty* turns.

There are, it is true, a number of obscurities in Mill's account, all
of which centre on the relationship between choice and the knowledge
of what makes for happiness or the good life in one's own case. So far
I have written as if there were a univocal notion of autonomy, which
Mill's writings exemplify. Such an impression could only be seriously
misleading. Rather, we discover in a range of writers, and even within
the writings of a single thinker, a whole continuum of conceptions. At
one extreme, we find in Spinoza a conception of autonomy which
might be called 'closed', in that it implies that the fully autonomous
agent (if such there could be) could find uniquely determinate solutions
to all practical questions. On this view, moral and practical dilemmas
are each of them susceptible to resolution through the application of
reason, which (at least in principle) is fully capable of yielding a speci-
fication of the good life for man and, presumably, for each man. At
another extreme, there is in the writings of the early Sartre an 'open'
view of autonomy, in which the idea that reason may settle practical
questions is itself dismissed as expressive of a heteronomous 'spirit of
seriousness'.

Mill's own conception of autonomy, I suggest, is most nearly akin to
that adumbrated by Aristotle. As a number of commentators have
observed,[12] Mill's account of character as a cluster of 'habitual willings',
closely resembles Aristotle's account in the *Nicomachean Ethics*. One

80

major difference between the two accounts, however, is found in Mill's radical pluralism. Though, like Aristotle, he thinks that all human excellences will be informed or characterised by the exercise of generic human capacities, he differs from Aristotle in insisting on the unique- ness which will characterise any man's happiness, when it is taken as an 'organic whole'. A happy man will not, then, be simply a very distinct instance of a general type; rather, one part of his happiness, a necessary part, in Mill's view, will be that he has fulfilled the peculiar demands of his own nature. Note that Mill is not insisting on the truism that circumstances and accidents of individual endowment will limit or constrain any man's opportunities for the attainment of excellence. More, he is insisting that the nature that awaits actualisation has unique features. It is this latter claim which some writers have ridiculed as expressing a doctrine of 'the Sanctity of Idiosyncrasy'.[13] Apart from the pejorative tone of such an expression, those who use it are surely correct that it is Mill's view that autonomous men, each of whom is in search of his own nature, will be more different from one another the closer they come to responding to the demands of their individual natures. Clearly, given Mill's emphasis on a pluralism of individual natures, there are epistemological problems both in determining their outer boundaries of variation and in determining the narrow range of life-styles within which any man may hope to attain excellence.

A second area of difference between Mill's account of individuality and Aristotle's account of human flourishing is located in Mill's insis- tence that choice-making is a necessary ingredient of the good life for any man. On some interpretations of Aristotle's view of practical deliberation, at any rate, the role of choice would be that of a means to the good life: it would not be even partly constitutive of it. There is indeed a tension in Mill between the cognitivist overtones of his talk of 'experiments in living' and the moral voluntarism intimated in some parts of his exposition of the elements of individuality. Some hard questions suggest themselves. Must a man whose desires and projects are his own, who displays authenticity, be autonomous? (Might he not just stumble on a form of life which fulfils his unique nature?) True, a man in whom the generic capacities of choice-making and so on are un- developed will not attain the full happiness of which he is capable as a human being. On the other hand, certain kinds of self-knowledge connected with autonomy might actually obstruct the flowering of a man's unique capacities and gifts. (Think of the creative artist whose work withers after psychoanalysis.) There is here a significant area of

difficulty for Mill's conception of happiness and of the place of individuality in it.

Again, at times, as I have myself observed in my discussion of Mill's theory of morality, Mill moves bewilderingly between the perspective of the practical agent and that of the detached observer. On some views of practical knowledge, it might seem that an experiment in living could yield knowledge only to the committed partisan, the agent actively involved in its undertakings. On other views, just the opposite would be true.

Unsurprisingly, we find no explicit treatment of these problems in Mill. We may conjecture that the role of choice-making for Mill derives in part from his conviction that many goods are such only if they are chosen, and, also, perhaps, from a conviction that, whereas the unique elements of any individual's character are given to him by nature, their achieving any kind of organic unity can only be the product of recurrent choice-making.[14] We may express what was perhaps Mill's view on these questions in the idiom of open and closed conceptions of autonomy I adopted earlier, by saying that Mill's own conception was probably only partly a closed one. Given the absence in Mill's writings of any sustained consideration of these questions, such an interpretation is reasonable, but it is not the only one supportable by the evidence.

The preceding discussion may enable us to restate more precisely the relationship between Mill's theory of individuality, his philosophical psychology and his argument for liberty. Mill always emphasises the presence of an active element in the mind: both in the formal discussions of psychology, and in the occasional writings, such as the essays on poetry, Mill rejected the view of the mind as purely receptive of external impressions. Similarly, according to Mill, happiness was to be found in activity: it was not, as he put it, 'a collective something' which might be considered as 'swelling any aggregate',[15] but rather the form of life expressing each man's own nature. Again, recall Mill's argument that to suppose that men can be happy without the exercise of their active faculties is to confuse the two ideas of happiness and contentment.[16] On occasion, Mill comes close to embracing a kind of moral individualism, in which the notion of well-being or happiness loses all sense except as an abstract term applied to the objects of any sort of human striving. It is not, indeed, wholly an abstract term, since Mill thinks it to be a fact that individuals will tend to converge on forms of life which have some shared characteristics. It is, indeed, this latter belief which creates some difficulties for Mill. For, if I have described his utilitarianism as hierarchical and pluralistic, it is plain that Mill needs some account of how conflicts are to be settled, when the various elements of utility make competing demands; and this is not to be found in his writings. What is clear, however, is that Mill denies that anyone can achieve happiness or the good life, unless he has his own conception of happiness; and the diversity of legitimate conceptions of happiness is grounded in the plurality of individual natures.

A major question for the Doctrine of Liberty has to do with the authority Mill claims for his view of human nature. As an empiricist, Mill is compelled to build his theory of men on the evidences of observation and experiment. In the *System of Logic* Mill had advanced the project of an empirical science of ethology, which would uncover the laws of development of human character. Mill's own failure to contribute to this science (which we recognise now as an earlier version of social psychology) was a source of disappointment and embarrassment to him, and not without reason. It was on the basis of the laws of ethology that the various precepts of the Art of Life were to be grounded, and scepticism about the possibility of a progressive science of morals and politics founded on human nature – a scepticism to which Macaulay had given biting expression in his attack on James Mill's *Essay on Government* – at last confounded. Unfortunately, Mill came up with no candidates for laws of ethology, so that the Doctrine of Liberty (along with the rest of the Art of Life) lacks the empirical foundation in scientific knowledge of man and society he wanted to give it.

Mill was not himself successful, then, in linking the Art of Life with the laws of ethology, and in our assessment of the plausibility of Mill's view of man we must draw on whatever theoretical and common-sensical beliefs about human nature we put our store in. The absence in Mill's larger philosophy of a scientific foundation for the Art of Life does not show that such a basis cannot be supplied. A fundamental objection to the consistency of Mill's philosophy and, indirectly, to the utilitarian credentials of the Doctrine of Liberty, concerns the question whether the view of human nature presupposed by *On Liberty* is empiricist at all. It might be urged that, not only Mill's affinities with Aristotle on the nature of happiness, but the teleological language of *On Liberty* and the *a priori* character of much of Mill's moral psychology, show him to be working with an essentialist rather than an empiricist conception of man. This is to say that Mill did not take the evidences of human behaviour as decisive for a statement of man's essential attributes, which might be more or less revealed in human conduct. The difficulty, of course, is that Mill's empiricist theory of knowledge seems to close this option for Mill. How might this difficulty be coped with?

In part, the idea that there are human essences or natures poses no problem for Mill, even though his empiricist outlook is uncongenial to essentialist language. I have already suggested that Mill absorbed the Romantic belief that each man possessed a peculiar and in-born endowment which might or might not be realised in the course of his life. This belief does not overthrow Mill's empiricism, so long as the identification of any man's essence or nature remains a matter of observation and experiment. But can the notion of an individual nature or essence itself be given an empiricist interpretation? I cannot see that the difficulty here is fatal for Mill. As Stuart Hampshire has observed, discussing Spinoza's idea of freedom:[17]

> The notion of an individual nature or essence may be found altogether obscure. We can, I think, still attach a sense to the notion of the essential characteristics of a species, and to the judgement of individuals as more or less perfect specimens of their kinds. But can we intelligibly speak of an individual or particular thing becoming more or less of an individual? Spinoza provides a criterion by which the approach to perfection of an individual qua individual is to be judged: the criterion is the degree to which the individual is active and self-determining.

My argument here is that, so long as we allow Mill the notion of an individual endowment open to discovery by observation and experiments in living, the rationalist or essentialist idiom of individual essences or natures can be given an empiricist translation. Whether or not empirical investigation bears out the claims of the theory of higher pleasures, and thereby supports the Doctrine of Liberty, is a question I take up in the last chapter of this book. At this stage I wish only to remark that, apart from the claim that individuals have natures or essences, Mill makes no claim about the general properties of human nature. The psychological laws he mentions are, in fact almost wholly abstract and formal, all of them being reducible to the law of association of ideas itself. Much of Mill's informal discussion of questions in morals and politics suggests that he thought human nature to be susceptible to almost unlimited variation and modification, so that the idea of a species-nature for man (apart from that given by his biological constitution) had little application for Mill. At times, though, Mill was attracted by a paradoxical version of essentialism, according to which the indefinite alterability of human nature is itself to be explained by the power, rooted in reflexive thought, which men have to make experiments on themselves. It is this view of human nature, more than any other, that is consonant with the argument of *On Liberty*. I will turn to it, and consider its status and uses in Mill, in the last chapter of this book. The obvious question is whether *this* essentialist thesis about man can be given an empirical defence.

The theory of human nature presupposed by *On Liberty* can be restated, then, as follows: According to this theory, human beings are understood to be engaged in recurrently revising the forms of life and modes of experience which they have inherited, and by which 'human nature' itself is constituted in any given time and place. In this account of man as a creature engaged in an endless process of self-transformation, what distinguishes human beings from members of other animal species is only their powers of reflexive thought and deliberate choice by which indeterminacy enters into human thought and action (together with the properties involved in having a more or less unalterable biological constitution). In such an account again, no statement claiming universal validity can be made about the attributes of human nature, save that it is essentially indeterminate, and so open to improvement in indefinitely many divergent directions. It is this conception of man, in which radical uncertainty of human nature constitutes the human species, that coheres most naturally with *On Liberty*. If this conception of human nature is imputed to Mill, it becomes intelligible why Mill saw progress, not in terms of the mass manufacture of any one type of human being, but as the promotion of the growth of the powers and capacities of autonomous thought and action. It is the growth of these powers which allows the cultivation of diverse excellences or forms of self-development, elevates the character of human wants, and fosters cultural and social development in 'innumerable divergent directions' by facilitating 'experiments of living'.

As I have reconstructed it, the argument of *On Liberty* is that social freedom (which I have taken to comprehend both legal liberty and immunity from the penalties and pressures of public opinion) is to be ranked over other goods because the promotion of a diversity of styles of life and modes of thought is partly constitutive of man's development as an autonomous agent. In *On Liberty*, then, social progress cannot be conceived of apart from the promotion of liberty. As Mill puts it:[18]

85

> The spirit of improvement is not always a spirit of liberty, for it
> may aim at forcing improvements on an unwilling people; and the
> spirit of liberty, insofar as it resists such attempts, may ally itself
> locally and temporarily with the opponents of improvement; but the
> only unfailing and permanent source of improvement is liberty, since
> by it there are as many possible independent centres of improvement
> as there are individuals.

So, if it is true that man's powers of reflexive thought prevent anything in man's social life from ever being fixed, finished or closed, then
progress will consist in the open-ended transformation of the forms of
man's social life along with a search (equally interminable) for the
weaknesses, incoherences and other inadequacies in his understanding
of the forms of his life. This is an essentialist view of human nature
according to which, paradoxically, the essence of man is identified
in the discovery that man lacks any determinate generic nature such as
is possessed by material objects and by unreflective creatures. It is a
paradoxical version of essentialism, also, in that the indeterminacy
characterising mankind as a species is qualified by the discoverable
essence in which Mill believes each member of the human species to
be peculiar. Mill's theory of individuality, then, combines the claim that
man is his own maker with the claim that, for each man, a nature exists
which awaits discovery. Mill's thesis is that a happy human life requires
the recurrent making of choices because only choice-making can weld
into an organic whole the diverse and possibly competing demands of
a man's nature. A fundamental question arises here as to whether this
view of human happiness is not thoroughly ideal-regarding and, if so,
whether this opens a fatal breach with anything recognisable as utilitarianism.

3 WANTS AND IDEALS IN THE DOCTRINE OF LIBERTY

Many of Mill's critics have accused him of bolstering the doctrine of
liberty with an aprioristic moral psychology for which there is little
independent justification. Certainly, a measure of circularity would
enter his doctrine if it could be shown that his conception of happiness merely encapsulates his moral ideals in other terms. So far as
his own view of the matter is concerned, Mill's position is reasonably
clear. There can be little doubt that Mill believed that, given an

appropriate range of relevant experience, men would in fact prefer activities involving the exercise of their best powers of discrimination and judgment over activities that do not. Mill is not committed to the view that men always display this preference — he is not bound to hold to the absurd view that, as between beer-drinking and wine-bibbing, men who know both always favour the latter on the ground of its greater demands of discrimination on the palate; but he is committed to the view that a preference for activities involving the exercise of autonomous thought and of capacities of imagination and discrimination will dominate the lives of experienced judges.

Mill's position in this area may still seem unpersuasive or unclear to many readers. Indeed, many of Mill's more recent critics have found it so. In his able critique of Millian liberalism, Haksar has argued that Mill cleaves to a high-minded conception of the good dependent on a certain ideal of the person: Mill's doctrine, he maintains, 'does not commit him to giving equal status to all forms of life', even though the identification of higher forms of life involves Mill in making perfectionist judgments which his official utilitarian theory disallowed.[19] Again, Mill's conception of happiness may still seem open to the objection, urged by Finnis,[20] against all forms of consequentialism, that it entails making comparable what are strictly incommensurable goods: it is bound to try to rank along a single scale values for which there is no common measure. Most crucially, perhaps, it might be urged that Mill's belief that there is a determinate class of higher pleasures is in conflict with his belief in the indefinite diversity of human nature: he cannot have it both ways. Either his doctrine of the higher pleasures supports his theory of liberty only because it already embodies a liberal preference for certain kinds of personality (in which case it gives no independent reason in favour of the Principle of Liberty) or else it rests on assumptions in empirical psychology and sociology which may well be false. What is there to be said in response to these criticisms?

The first of these objections, best put by Haksar, submits that Mill's underlying moral theory is perfectionist. By this is meant (following Rawls) that it is concerned primarily with the promotion of a certain type of human excellence, and only secondarily with want-satisfaction. The perfectionist theory is a species of maximising consequentialism, but not a want-regarding sort. If the attribution to Mill of this sort of ideal-regarding conception[21] were sound, it would indeed be a serious blow to his Doctrine of Liberty, which aims to have persuasive force even for those attached to illiberal ideals of character. But I cannot see that it has force. In the first place, the perfectionist character of a moral outlook is a matter of degree. A perfectionist moral code (one which attached great weight to considerations to do with personal excellence) may incorporate very specific precepts about behaviour, or else it may be more or less open-ended. No doubt Mill himself favoured persons of an adventurous, generous, open-minded disposition over timid, mean-spirited and narrow-minded types, but his argument as to the value of liberty is intended to have force for both. Mill's conception of the good life may be perfectionist in the sense that it ranks lives which are in large measure self-chosen over those that are customary, but this is a procedural perfectionism rather than a full theory of the good life. In weighting autonomy and security heavily in any scheme of human welfare, and giving priority to autonomy once certain conditions have been satisfied, Mill does work with what Rawls has termed a thin theory of the good — a minimalist conception of human welfare expressed in terms of a theory of vital interests or primary goods.[22] Operating with such a reference to the minimum conditions of the full achievement of human well-being does not by itself go any distance towards making Mill a perfectionist. Indeed, Mill's own claim is that those who are used to making their own choices will not easily or lightly abandon this practice, and this is an empirical claim, a wager of sorts, rather than an affirmation of an ideal. If Mill never faced the possibility that men would freely give up their liberty, this is because he thought he had good reason to believe the advantages of liberty were self-reinforcing. To argue that Mill was mistaken about this, even if the argument were incontrovertibly sound, would not support the very different claim that his real moral theory is perfectionist.

The two latter objections are in several respects more substantial. Mill acknowledged that each man's conception of his own happiness would most likely include competing elements, but he offered no guidance as to how these conflicts were to be settled: this is a point to which I shall return when I come to appraise his doctrine taken as a whole. Is his conviction of the diversity of human nature in conflict with his account of the higher pleasures? I cannot see how: Mill's criteria of a higher pleasure were that it be chosen after a process of autonomous thought and choice and that it express the unique demands of the individual's own nature. This pair of conditions excludes many pleasures while still leaving an infinite variety of intellectual and other pleasures in the field. There is nothing inconsistent in Mill holding that some pleasures can be known to fail the two tests I have mentioned whereas there may at the same time be novel pleasures, as yet unknown, which pass them. Some pleasures, it is true, may conceivably be autonomously chosen as in accordance with the individual's own nature and yet involve a relinquishment of autonomy. Mill's view on this possibility, I take it, is not an *a priori* one: he does not seek to defeat it as a possibility, but rather to suggest its improbability or rarity. This may be a modest position, but it is not an absurd one. Mill is committed to the proposition that men who have tasted the advantages and pleasures of liberty will not trade them away for other benefits: he holds, as an empirical matter, the belief that the condition of liberty is in this respect irreversible.

It is not immediately clear what sort of evidence Mill would accept as overturning his beliefs in this area. Nor, indeed, is it at all clear what evidence it would be reasonable for Mill to accept in this connection. In the last section of the final chapter of this book I will make some observations on this difficult question. At this stage, I want only to remark that, provided Mill's prediction holds up in the generality of cases, there is nothing ideal-regarding in his conception of happiness. Mill is not holding to a perfectionist ethic in which the promotion of an ideal of human excellence is to be undertaken even if it competes with want-satisfaction. His view is, rather, that human happiness depends upon a certain sort of stability of character. The crucial question is, however, whether Mill holds to an ideal of personality independent of its contribution to general want-satisfaction. There is no historical or textual evidence that he did, and conjectures about what he would think were his expectations about human development confounded are excessively speculative. Though it is not the case that Mill's doctrine could be overturned by the odd case of a contented sloth, it is avowedly vulnerable to the test of human experience. Thus it can claim for itself only that it represents a not unreasonable wager. It is defeasible by experience and criticisable by the evidence of life — a point to which I will have occasion to return. One aspect of this criticism, though, is in the area of applications of Mill's Principle of Liberty, and it is to some of the most important of these that I now turn.

V

APPLICATIONS

---

1 PATERNALISM

It is worth noting right at the start of any examination of Mill's account of state paternalism that it is a presupposition of any principle of paternalism (and so of all discussion of moral problems generated by paternalism) that a meaningful distinction can indeed be drawn between behaviour that is (at least mainly and directly) self-regarding and behaviour that is other-regarding. For, however such a distinction might be drawn, there can be no distinct moral problem regarding paternalism unless it can be made in some significant form or other, since (supposing any distinction of this kind to be illegitimate or misconceived) all 'paternalistic' invasions of liberty can be justified as necessary for the protection of the welfare of persons other than those whose liberty has been restricted. In that case, no restriction of liberty would ever be (wholly or mainly) paternalistic, so there could never be a genuine moral dilemma as to whether it is proper to coerce an individual solely in his own interest. Hence, all discussion about paternalism is logically or conceptually parasitic on the possibility of making a distinction analogous to that which Mill wishes to make between self-regarding and other-regarding actions. In specifying harm to others as a necessary condition of justified restriction of liberty, the Principle of Liberty disqualifies an indefinitely large range of reasons as sufficient to support such restriction, among which paternalist considerations are important.

The principle of legal paternalism justifies state coercion to protect individuals from self-inflicted harm or (more stringently) to induce individuals to act in ways beneficial to themselves. The anti-paternalist implication of Mill's principle stipulates that no one (state or society) can legitimately interfere with the fully voluntary choice of a mature rational agent concerning matters which affect only or primarily his own interests. As Mill famously puts it:[1]

> [A man's] own good, either physical or moral, is not sufficient warrant [for liberty-limitation]. He cannot rightfully be compelled to do or forbear because it will be better for him to do so, because it will make him happier, because, in the opinion of others, to do so would be wise, or even right. . . . Over himself, over his own body and mind, the individual is sovereign.

Mill conceives of his principle as allowing the state and society to limit a man's liberty so as to protect him from the damaging consequences of his own ignorance or delusion, wherever the circumstances of the case give good reason for supposing that his uninformed or misinformed choice did not correspond to the choice he would have made had he understood clearly the situation in which he found himself. Equally plainly, all such counterfactual propositions, where they are not testable by a direct appeal to the testimony of the agent of whom the course of action is predicated, rest upon some general theoretical account of what are normal or typical human responses in the circumstances specified. This, and other qualifications which Mill explicitly makes to his 'absolute' proscription of paternalism disclose part of the rationale of his general repudiation of paternalism and also specify some of the reasons for his departures from this general position. In a famous passage, Mill declares:[2]

> If either a public officer or anyone else saw a person attempting to cross a bridge which had been ascertained to be unsafe, and there was no time to warn him of his danger, they might seize him and turn him back, without any real infringement of his liberty, for liberty consists in doing what one desires, and he does not desire to fall into the river.

It is Mill's view that a person may be protected, not only from the consequences of his ignorance and misinformation, but also from various other conditions which render his choices (even when they are fully and correctly informed) less clearly autonomous. An individual may be 'a child, or delirious, or in some state of excitement, incompatible with the full use of the reflecting faculty'.[3] These remarks commit

Mill to a weak form of paternalism, according to which state and society may legitimately restrict liberty so as to prevent harmful self-regarding conduct when it is clearly not the result of considered rational deliberation.

This weak form of paternalism to which Mill subscribes typically requires no more than a temporary liberty-limiting intervention on the part of state and society, aimed at establishing whether or not the self-damaging conduct was clearly autonomous, and, if not, to prevent the agent from acting until he becomes (or becomes once again) capable of autonomous thought and action. This weak form of paternalism would not normally be consistent with the permanent imposition of a limit to liberty, or with any unqualified proscription of self-damaging actions.

Mill appears to commit himself to a stronger, more substantial form of paternalism in his discussion of irreversibly liberty-limiting contracts. In *Principles of Political Economy* he contends that the state should not facilitate or enforce irrevocable contracts,[4] while in *On Liberty* he maintains that the state should in no way recognise or enforce a contract of voluntary servitude:[5]

> In this and most civilised countries . . . an engagement by which a person should sell himself, or allow himself to be sold, as a slave would be null and void, neither enforced by law, nor by opinion. The ground of thus limiting his power of voluntarily disposing of his own lot in life is apparent, and very clearly seen in this extreme case. The reason for not interfering, unless for the sake of others, with a person's voluntary acts, is consideration for his liberty. His voluntary choice is evidence that what he chooses is desirable, or at least endurable to him, and his own good is on the whole best provided for by allowing him to take his own means of pursuing it. But, by selling himself for a slave, he abdicates his liberty; he foregoes any future use of it beyond the single act. He therefore defeats, in his own case, the very purpose which is the justification of allowing him to dispose of himself. He is no longer free; but henceforth in a position which has no longer the presumption in its favour that would be afforded by his voluntarily remaining in it. The principle of freedom cannot require that he should not be free. It is not freedom to be allowed to alienate his freedom . . . there are perhaps no contracts or engagements, except those that relate to money or money's worth, of which one can venture to say that there ought to be no liberty whatever of retraction.

Does Mill's stand on the question of servitude involve him in any inconsistency? Does it, in particular, involve any abridgment of the Principle of Liberty? Two views are possible here, in one of which Mill is consistent whereas in the other he is not. Let us take first the argument for his consistency.[6] It is urged to begin with that, while it is true that the Principle of Liberty entails or presupposes a principle against paternalism, what the Principle of Liberty disqualifies is the *coercive* limitation of liberty. Though the Principle of Liberty is argued for by appeal to its role in safeguarding other sorts of freedom, its subject-matter is only freedom from coercion. The anti-paternalist principle it entails is, then, a principle which forbids only coercive action to prevent men from harming themselves. But, and this is the second point, no coercion is involved in refusing to make a contractual or quasi-contractual agreement enforceable. Such refusal may, indeed, limit the autonomy which the Principle of Liberty serves to promote, but refusal of this sort is not forbidden by the Principle of Liberty itself.

If the non-enforcement of a contract of voluntary servitude does not fall under the Principle of Liberty, by what principle of Mill's Doctrine of Liberty is it supported? Simply by the Principle of Utility (when taken in conjunction with expediency). Mill's view is clearly that the question of which agreements ought to be made contractually binding, and in what measure, is answerable only by appeal to utility. That utility would on balance be lost by making contracts of slavery enforceable needs little argument. The counter-example of the man whose welfare is on balance promoted by entering into an enforceable slave contract is not forceful. For the welfare protected by refusal to facilitate or enable the enforcement of slave contracts is not the agent's own, but the general welfare. It was Mill's belief that the importance of autonomy and individuality as necessary ingredients in well-being tended systematically to be neglected. Since an enormous bureaucracy instituted to ascertain the full voluntariness and to monitor waiting periods of candidates for voluntary slavery would be cumbersome, costly and probably inefficient, any institution embodying a weak policy of paternalism must be disqualified on the utilitarian ground of wastefulness. On the other hand, if liberty is indeed one of the most underrated of the necessary ingredients of utility, then a policy that is wholly permissive with regard to willing slavery will be rejected inasmuch as it may tend to support a general disregard for the value of liberty. On this basis only a blanket policy of non-enforcement remains in the field.

Now arguments of this kind, cogent as they are, do not seem to be sufficiently forceful to support the tone of Mill's language in the passage I have quoted, and it is not wholly clear, therefore, that they establish Mill's consistency. This has led one commentator[7] to contend that, when he comes to consider the case of the willing slave, Mill abandons a utility-maximising approach for a liberty-maximising paternalism. Now if Mill thinks utility or happiness contains freedom or liberty, but contains other things as well, then this interpretation must be rejected. For the other ingredients of well-being must on occasion compete with and trump liberty and autonomy, unless we are prepared (as Mill certainly was not) to resort to the desperate expedient of according autonomy an infinite weight against all other ingredients of well-being. In any case, this interpretation is unacceptably paradoxical for it is manifest that coercively preventing a man from irreversibly giving up his freedom where doing so promotes his interests is not paternalism (since by hypothesis it does not protect his interests) but a species of legal moralism. It will be a species of legal moralism if the principal value is that of liberty and if it is also true (as it is true in the case I have hypothesised) that his liberty has a subordinate place in the willing slave's interests. Nor are the paradoxical aspects of this interpretation weakened by invoking the metaphor of earlier and later selves.[8] Even if it does sometimes make sense to individuate several selves or personalities within a single lifetime, protecting a later from an earlier self seems to be prevention of 'harm to others' rather than any sort of paternalism.

As against these arguments, counter-arguments seem to me to be available which go far to show Mill's consistency in the case of willing slavery. I have already noted (as an argument in support of Mill's consistency on this question) that the Principle of Liberty does not itself positively promote autonomy, but only removes some of the coercive impediments to autonomy. This point holds even if we are ready (as I think we should be ready) to see the Principle as regulating moral coercion by public opinion as well as legal coercion, for even in such a reading, the force of the Principle would still only be that it removes an important class of obstacles to autonomy. The Principle is not breached by anyone's refraining from facilitating autonomous choice and action. Even if refusing to facilitate enforcement of slave contracts did abridge autonomy, it might still promote autonomy: an abridgment of a value does not annihilate it and might even maximise it. The curtailment of autonomy involved in non-enforcement of some contracts might be defensible as a maximising curtailment. Again, whereas Mill does not hold that a man's interest in autonomy always trumps all his other interests, he does think that where he has a reasonable prospect of attaining autonomy, that is his weightiest interest and ought in general to override his other interests. Men whose circumstances are so bad that a contract of voluntary servitude looks attractive will not typically be in a good position to weight their interest in autonomy against their other interests, and they will often make mistaken calculations. Even if a man's interests were maximally promoted by a contract of willing slavery, that would not settle the issue in favour of facilitating such a contract for him. For it is not his interest alone, but the general interest, that Mill as a utilitarian is bound to consult. General neglect of the importance of autonomy as a necessary ingredient in human well-being supports a general policy of according it priority in the circumstances with which Mill is concerned. Thus, whereas a non-enforcement policy is not forbidden by the Principle of Liberty, it can be supported by reasons to do with the promotion of happiness. A non-enforcement policy of this kind remains paternalistic, to be sure, inasmuch as it is supported by reference to the interests of a typical agent. It is not exclusively or predominantly a paternalistic policy, however, and the paternalism it expresses is of the very weak variety that consists in not positively facilitating or enabling agents to act on their current wishes. This latter sort of paternalism is the only one Mill admits in his discussion of irreversibly liberty-limiting contracts in his *Principles of Political Economy*. And when Mill comes to discuss the voluntary servitude (as he saw it) embodied in the marriage contract of his time in the last chapter of his *Subjection of Women*,[9] he invoked as the decisive consideration against such contracts their degrading effect on the moral atmosphere of society and so upon the general interest.

Mill's objection to paternalism, together with his admission of a weak form of paternalism in extremis, may thus become both intelligible and justifiable, if we impute to him the view that protection of an individual's own interests cannot supply a sufficient warrant for restricting his liberty, since the interests of an individual considered in the circumstances where the Principle of Liberty applies cannot typically be promoted by restricting his liberty. This is so because, weightier than any of his other interests, the individual has an interest in becoming or remaining an autonomous agent. It is true, of course, that coercive interventions, along with other restrictions of liberty, may be among the empirically necessary conditions of the growth in an individual of the powers and capacities involved in autonomous thought and action. This is, indeed, a truth which Mill explicitly acknowledges when he asserts (in the introductory chapter of *On Liberty*) that the Principle of Liberty has no application until men 'have become capable of being improved by free and equal discussion'. 'Until then' he delcares 'there is nothing for them but implicit obedience to an Akbar or a Charlemagne, if they are so fortunate as to find one.'[10] While Mill is ready to admit − and, indeed, emphatically asserts − that coercion may be among the conditions empirically necessary to the growth of the capacities of an autonomous agent, he is equally insistent that, in civilised societies, and in all but the rarest cases, men's growth as autonomous agents is best promoted by according them liberty. Only by encouraging men to exercise their powers as choosers and reasoners in a choice environment undistorted by coercive interventions can we expect that they will develop into autonomous agents: for 'the mental and moral, like the muscular powers, are improved only by being exercised'.[11] In addition to these quasi-empirical claims for the educative values of liberty, it is a feature of the concept of autonomy which I impute to Mill that autonomous action cannot intelligibly be supposed to be action under coercion. His autonomy is abridged by coercion, even if the abridgment maximises his autonomy on balance. Accordingly, while a man may well best approach the status of an autonomous agent if his liberty is restricted at critical junctures in his life (and especially in childhood) so as to inculcate in him the skills and aptitudes characteristic of an autonomous agent, it reflects a misconception of the nature of autonomy to suppose that autonomous action itself could be secured by coercion.

The pattern of Mill's argument against paternalism may be displayed in the form of three premises. First, Mill ascribes to each man a weighty interest in becoming an autonomous agent, making this ascription part of a characterisation of the qualities of mind and character comprising human happiness. Second, Mill's argument presupposes the logical truth that action cannot be autonomous if the decision to act is made under coercion. Third, Mill advances the empirical conjecture that the other defining features of autonomous agency − features of rationality, critical reflection and strength of will, for example − are in general most efficaciously promoted by applying the principle of liberty and encouraging men to undertake 'experiments of living'. This rational reconstruction of Mill's argument against paternalism renders intelligible and legitimate Mill's standpoint in the limiting case of voluntary servitude. The supreme justifying value by appeal to which Mill supports his prohibition of paternalism — the vital interest in autonomous agency — dictates a very weak form of paternalism where the possibility of the individual forfeiting irrevocably his prospects of autonomy is itself in question. On this question, Mill's view seems to be plausible as well as consistent with the rest of his doctrine. Mill's arguments in this area take for granted that paternalist and moralistic interventions may be distinguished, and this is an assumption that some may wish to dispute. It is to this question that I now turn in the context of a general consideration of Mill's views on legal and social moralism.

2 MORALISM

As I have interpreted it, the Principle of Liberty may be restated as stipulating that the liberty of the individual ought to be restricted only if his actions are injurious to the vital interests of others, where it is understood to be every man's weightiest interest that he comes to be an autonomous agent. The Principle rules out as illegitimate the legal enforcement of the positive moral principles of the community, and indeed licenses the state in acting to prevent the enforcement, by public opinion, of the dictates of positive morality. Only the protection of the vital interests can justify restriction of liberty, whether by society or the state. As I have intimated at an earlier phase of my account, Mill's Doctrine of Liberty (via the theory of vital interests) grounds a theory of moral rights. It then becomes the thesis that each man may legitimately claim from society that he be protected in the enjoyment both of the freedoms of action which are logically necessary conditions of autonomy and of the immunities and securities that are empirically necessary conditions of the growth of the capacities characteristic of an autonomous agent, whenever meeting such a claim would on balance promote the attainment of human well-being (conceived of as a state of flourishing supervenient on the development of generically human powers of autonomous thought and action). The domain of freedom of action protected by the principle of liberty, deontologically described but teleologically justified, equals the sum of moral rights defining the liberal society defended in *On Liberty*. These moral or personal rights to freedom are enumerated by Mill when he characterises 'the appropriate region of human liberty' as comprising, first, 'the inward domain of consciousness', which he judges to be connected inseparably with freedom of expression; second, liberty of tastes and pursuits; and third, freedom of association.[12]

My contention is that exercise of any of the liberties comprehended within these general categories of freedom of action partly constitutes the form of life of an autonomous agent, so that a free society is to be understood as a society of free men. Further, I claim that the domain of morality (as distinct from prudence and aesthetics) is circumscribed by Mill in terms of respect for persons as bearers of capacities for autonomous thought and action. The moral point of view, then, is that which is concerned with the protection of human interests, where these are constituted partly by states of affairs logically or empirically necessary for the attainment of autonomy, partly by the counterfactual preferences that may reasonably be imputed to autonomous agents.

What is the relation between this quasi-Kantian formulation for the definition of morality in terms of respect for persons and the domain of aesthetic considerations marked out by the theory of the Art of Life? The answer to this question is to be found in the truth that, while autonomy (in that it is a necessary constituent of human well-being) partly constitutes any form of human self-development, the range of human performances and involvements in respect of which talk of excellences or higher pleasures is appropriate remains none the less indefinitely large (though not entirely indeterminate). For, while the exercise of powers of autonomous thought and action is a logically necessary condition of the display of any human excellence, the autonomous character of any human activity is not on this account a criterion of its worthiness, since it is nowhere claimed that the exercise of the powers of an autonomous agent is also a logically sufficient condition of his displaying a human excellence.

My general submission is that it is with the virtues, graces and excellences characteristic of definite forms of life that aesthetic appraisal is concerned in Mill's theory of the Art of Life. Admittedly, since I have stipulated that autonomy is a necessary constituent of every kind of self-development, and since I claim that this stipulation accords with Mill's use of such cognate terms as 'originality' and 'individuality', I have claimed that the domain of human well-being as a whole is bounded by the exercise of powers of autonomous thought and action. Within this indefinitely large range of forms of life open to an autonomous agent, there are many recognisable forms of life – some, no doubt, as yet unexplored – each of which has its own canons of worthiness. It is these latter standards of excellence and respect-worthiness which I understand Mill to be excluding from the domain of morality and so of enforceability when he characterises them as encompassing considerations of aesthetics or nobility. It is to excellences characteristic of some definite ideal of life chosen from among all the ways of life accessible to an autonomous agent that Mill is referring when he denies that men have duties to themselves:[13]

> What are called duties to ourselves are not socially obligatory, unless circumstances render them at the same time duties of others. The term duty to oneself, when it means anything more than prudence, means self-respect or self-development, and for none of these is any one accountable to his fellow creatures, because for none of them is it for the good of mankind that he be held accountable to them.

This repudiation of a duty to develop oneself expresses the necessary truth that none of the excellences open to an autonomous agent can be promoted by the use of coercion, that is by restricting liberty. Since it is a feature of the valuable activities open to an autonomous agent — such as those involved in the cultivation of friendship, the pursuit of knowledge, religious devotion and the creation and contemplation of beauty — that they cannot be undertaken under the constraint of force or coercion, the impropriety of enforcement of 'aesthetic' criteria assumes the character of a logical prohibition rather than a substantive value judgment. Since the attributes of nobility cannot intelligibly be supposed to be displayed as products of force or coercion, the enforcement of standards of worthiness becomes simply incoherent, or at least self-defeating. Mill's rejection of enforcement of the criteria of excellence definitive of specific forms of life is, accordingly, dictated by his characterisation of morality. Evidence in support of this interpretation can be adduced by appeal to Mill's treatment of paradigm problems of legal moralism, such as those connected with prostitution and gambling, where his sole concern is seen to be not the suppression of any kind of activity judged to be disgraceful according to the standards expressing any normatively specific form of life, but rather the restriction of the liberty of those (such as casino owners and brothel keepers) who may be thought to have vested interest in exploiting the weakness of will (and so subverting the autonomy) of others. Mill's opposition to any enforcement of the claims of positive morality (where this cannot be justified by appeal to the interests of others) can be shown, similarly, to flow from a recognition that there are excellences whose flourishing requires a sphere of non-interference in which 'experiments of living' may be made which are safe from the invasive attentions of state and society. Once again, Mill's repudiation of enforcement in the domains of aesthetics and prudence is a strict implication of his account of morality as being in its nature enforceable and as largely consisting in respect for the autonomy of other persons.

The general policy of promoting autonomy implies prohibiting the enforcement of aesthetics and prudential standards – an implication strict enough for policies of enforcement in respect of these standards to be regarded as incoherent or at least self-defeating.

It may be thought that this reconstruction of Mill's argument begs several important questions. First of all, many writers have denied that policies of state paternalism and of legal moralism can be distinguished as easily and as uncontroversially as the interpretations I have advanced appear to presuppose. Second, many writers have asked why, if harm to others is the test for the legitimacy of intervention, the harm done to others through offence to their feelings does not count in the deliberation as to whether intervention is in the end warranted. Third, some of Mill's critics have asked whether the liberty or harm principle can plausibly apply only to assignable individuals. Must it not also apply to public institutions and to practices which serve the general welfare? Fourth, and finally, there are those who maintain that immorality is an intrinsically bad thing, whether or not it may be said to harm anyone in any straightforward, publicly testable fashion. Some who hold this view also hold that the badness of immorality sanctions liberty-restricting policies aimed at suppressing (or, at least, at deterring) it. It will be seen at once that each of these objections revives questions about 'harm', some of which I earlier canvassed.

Let us take these objections in reverse order. The fourth objection is one which Mill answers, it must be presumed, by invoking the theory of happiness as the only thing having intrinsic value. For, like the objector, Mill holds that wrongful conduct may always properly be subject to punishment. True, according to Mill, the fact that conduct violates the interests of others is never sufficient to justify making it punishable. Since even stringent punishment will rarely prevent wrongful conduct, the general aim is to deter it with the threat of sanctions. Unlike some advocates of a pure form of legal moralism, then, Mill would have no sympathy with a merely retributivist justification of punishment. Still, the objector and Mill are in agreement that the wrongfulness of an action creates a good reason for its punishability: they differ only in the primary area of what it is that makes conduct harmful and so wrong.

The third objection is somewhat harder to cope with. Mill plainly supports coercion in respect of the payment of taxes, and a number of forms of compulsory public service, where it would be fanciful to suppose that any individual's non-compliance would have any perceptible harmful effect on anyone. In the case of the peaceable individual who refuses to pay his taxes or to undertake jury service, it is not at all plausible to suggest that he does anything which causes harm to anyone. There are a number of rejoinders that Mill can (and, in some of his writings, does) make to objections like this. In respect of some natural duties (e.g. saving a drowning man at small risk to oneself), Mill supports a public opinion condemning deviation from minimally decent Good Samaritanism, and this on utilitarian grounds. Where such a public opinion exists, lapses from Good Samaritanism of the sort it prescribes will typically involve disappointment of reasonable expectations, and will accordingly be utilitarianly regrettable. Further, Mill argues in *Principles of Political Economy* that there are a number of goods, wanted by all or almost all, which will only be produced if all are required to contribute to defraying their cost. These are the public goods, which, in virtue of their indivisibility and non-excludability, cannot be charged for on a market basis. With respect to these goods, mutual coercion is the only workable means for producing them at all. Finally, there is in Mill an appeal to reciprocity or fairness as a condition of stable social co-operation, which justifies restricting liberty in order to sustain important social institutions. As I have earlier argued, however, Mill invokes a standard of equity in regard to institutions whose rationale is harm-prevention, and in which the protection of moral rights is grounded in vital interests.

At this point in my exposition, however, the second objection becomes unavoidable: what of the harm done to others through offence to their feelings? I have suggested earlier that it is as a maxim of utilitarian policy that Mill holds that the vital interests always take priority over the rest. Some very distinguished commentators, not unsympathetic to Mill, have maintained that the liberty principle by itself is too stringent, but must be constrained by an offence principle, distinct from the principle of legal moralism and from any principle about the prevention of harm to public institutions. Part of Mill's rather equivocal stance about some of the cases he discusses in the last chapter of *On*

Liberty seems to issue from his concern about 'offences against decency', or acts in 'violation of good manners'. It is impossible to discern in Mill's writings any clear account of how these offences are to be identified, and, clearly, if there are any such offences whose gravity warrants restriction of liberty, then Mill's interpreters are in a quandary.[14] For, in that case, either offence to feelings re-enters the class of utilities capable of being adduced to support a restriction of liberty, or else the liberty principle has been drastically abridged. The very casual and peremptory fashion in which Mill deals with this topic suggests to me that he thought it of little moment – 'only indirectly connected with our subject', as he puts it[15] – and it may be that his reason for this lay in a belief that liberty is not importantly restricted, when all that is proscribed is conduct in certain public places where offence to others is not readily avoidable. It must be admitted that this is a highly speculative suggestion, whose own merits are not large, and that Mill's writings are simply wanting in any adequate treatment of the problem.

Finally, can we reliably separate off cases of legal moralism from cases of state paternalism? Clearly, any theory according to which there may be 'moral harms' will make such a distinction difficult. We need to distinguish here between several different views about the concept of harm in its application to questions of paternalism and morality. At one extreme, we have the view that judgments about what is harmful and so any use of the concept of harm itself, are always internal to a specific moral outlook. Some who hold this view, like Phillipps and Mounce,[16] maintain that there may be and need be no common element in the things conceived of as harmful within different moral outlooks. This view seems too strong if it is offered as an account of all discourse in which the term 'harm' occurs. For there are non-moral uses of the term, and there are circumstances in which exponents of rival moralities may agree in their judgments as to what is harmful, but disagree in the judgments about what is to be done. A major weakness of this extreme view is that it would seem to allow no room for discussions of questions of prudential harm and benefit between people belonging to different moral practices. A less extreme view is that, since judgments about what is harmful are often informed by moral commitments and beliefs, we cannot reasonably expect them always to be uncontroversial and neutral as between competing moral outlooks. This view, by itself, poses no major threat to Mill's enterprise, since he may without difficulty acknowledge 'harm' to denote a relatively open-textured concept.

What he does is to argue for a rather restrictive conception of harm, in which it applies only to invasion of the vital interests: he advances this argument, not primarily as a conceptual anlaysis of 'harm' but chiefly as a utilitarianly grounded proposal about which harms are to be taken most seriously. Finally, it should be pointed out that someone who acknowledges that there may be 'moral harms' is not thereby committed to resist the anti-paternalist implications of the liberty principle. The difference between Mill and Hart[17] (on the one hand) and Devlin[18] and Fitzjames Stephen on the other is not primarily on the question of whether there may be harms of an irreducibly moral character. It is not even a difference as to whether morality may be enforced. Rather, it is a difference as to the content of morality itself, and a controversy as to the source of morality's authority. Primarily, however, it is a difference in assessment of the possibilities and limitations of human nature. For the 'disintegration theses'[19] of Devlin and Stephen, if they are empirical conjectures at all, are theories about the necessary conditions of social stability which Mill believed he had grounds for rejecting. Finally, it should be emphasised that, whereas Mill's doctrine disallows the coercive enforcement of positive morality, it does not rule out (and Mill himself sought to encourage[20]) the frank and forceful expression of opinion on questions of personal character and conduct. Though he does not seem to have supposed freedom in the expression of such opinions to be necessary to a stable social order, he would not have minded if (as his conservative critics suggest) it turns out to promote social stability.

3 FREEDOM OF EXPRESSION

It is true of any liberal theory of freedom of expression that it must account for the immunity from legal restriction of acts of expression which occasion manifest damage to interests of a gravity that would warrant such restriction if the acts were not acts of speech (for example) but acts of a non-expressive character. Mill acknowledges that acts of expression are in this respect a privileged class of acts in a number of passages:[21]

> Such being the reasons which make it imperative that human beings should be free to form opinions, and to express their opinions without reserve; and such the baneful consequences to the intellectual,

and through that to the moral nature of man, unless this liberty is either conceded, or asserted in spite of prohibition; let us next examine whether the same reasons do not require that men should be free to act upon their opinions — to carry them out in their lives, without hindrance, either physical or moral, from their fellow-men, so long as it is at their own risk and peril. This last proviso is of course indispensable. No one pretends that acts should be as free as opinions. On the contrary, even opinions lose their immunity when the circumstances in which they are expressed are such as to constitute their expression a positive instigation to some mischievous act.

In this passage Mill acknowledges that expressive acts enjoy a priviledged immunity from liberty-limiting legal restrictions on harm-preventing grounds. He allows to expressive acts a greater freedom from restriction on such grounds than other kinds of act. How might he justify this apparently unreasonable exemption? At the end of chapter two of *On Liberty*, Mill summarises the major arguments he has adduced in support of 'absolute freedom of opinion and sentiment on all subjects, practical or speculative, scientific, moral and theological'.[22] First, he appeals to the fact of human fallibility; second, he appeals to the value of truth; third, he appeals to the value of rationality, asserting that, even if an opinion contains the whole truth, it will be held as a prejudice, without understanding of its grounds in reason, if it is not challenged in open debate; and, fourth, he appeals to the value of vital belief, claiming that without 'the collision of adverse opinions', men's convictions lack the force of heartfelt views. In listing these four arguments in support of freedom of expression, Mill identifies two features that are partly constitutive of autonomous thought — the rationality and the vitality of the beliefs and judgments with which it operates — in the absence of which no man can attain 'the ideal perfection of human nature'. In making this reference to two constituents of autonomous thought, Mill resolves the paradox of any liberal theory of free expression: if it is legitimate to restrict non-expressive acts when they threaten damage to human interests, why is it illegitimate to restrict the liberty to perform expressive acts when they threaten similar damage (as surely they often do)? Mill's repudiation of restrictions on freedom of speech is a consistent application of his ascription to human beings of an overriding interest in becoming and remaining autonomous agents. Restrictions on free expression by their nature obstruct autonomous thought. For, provided always that the individual can be supposed to have attained 'the maturity of his faculties', it cannot coherently be suggested that he might forfeit his sovereignty in weighing rival reasons for action while continuing to regard himself as an autonomous agent. An autonomous agent who cherishes that status is obliged to discount both the harm to himself accruing from the acquisition of false beliefs and the harm done as a result of acquiring a belief (true or false) via an expressive act as being always overridden by the harm done by any restraint of free expression to the interest he shares with others in remaining an autonomous agent. While an autonomous agent may accept, accordingly, that the state has authority to subject him to various kinds of restraint, and while he may rely on the judgment of others about the rectitude of the state's imposing limits to his liberty, he cannot (without forfeiting his status as an autonomous agent) abrogate the responsibility he has to evaluate critically the state's actions and the judgments of others. Discharging the responsibility of an autonomous agent, however, presupposes that he possess all the resources of information and conflicting opinion and judgment which are indispensable conditions of rational deliberation and which can only be secured by the protection of liberal freedoms of speech. Such an interpretation of Mill's reasoning in support of freedom of speech is supported by the character of the famous exception which he allows to the principle of freedom of expression:[23]

> An opinion that corndealers are starvers of the poor, or that private property is robbery, ought to be unmolested when simply circulated through the press, but may justly incur punishment when delivered to an excited mob assembled before the house of a corndealer, and then handed about the same mob in the form of a placard.

It is surely possible to regard this passage as making an appeal to the improbability of autonomous thought in 'excited mobs' rather than an appeal to the harm to the interests of corndealers caused by the utterances made in such circumstances: for, after all, corndealers might be as severely harmed by confiscatory legislation (passed as a result of expressive acts uttered in the reasoned arguments of parliamentary debate) as by any sort of mob violence. Once again, the abridgments which Mill is prepared to make to his liberal principles disclose clearly the rationale for their general adoption — his overriding concern for the creation of a society of autonomous agents. Mill does not deny that expressive acts may be harmful; he insists that their harmfulness is not in general sufficient to warrant restricting them.

All this is not to say that there are no difficulties in Mill's theory of freedom of expression. Expressive acts are typically other-regarding and, in respect of some of them at least, a strong causal link can be established with harm to the vital interests of others. What of racist speech which directly engenders a lynching, for example? Within a right-based theory, it might make sense to maintain that, not incitement to violators of rights, but only rights violation, shall ever be punishable; but it is hard to see how such a view could be justifiable within a utilitarian outlook even of Mill's sort. As Marshall says of Mill's discussion of tyrannicide:[24]

> Mill says not only that the lawfulness of it may properly be discussed but that instigation to it in a particular case may be punished only if an overt act has followed and a probable connection can be established between the act and the instigation. This appears to mean some other overt act by someone other than the instigator and other than the act of instigation which may well be overt enough. Mill seems inconsistent here. What he presumably ought to be saying is that if an act is mischievous or damaging to others or to society, society may properly make it criminal and suppress such speech acts as are so closely connected with the commission of the act as to be part of it as to be counted as attempts to do the act; but that something to be called discussion, advocacy, debate, or expression of opinions about its desirability, can never be deemed to be part of a mischievous action in this sense.

What Mill lacks, in short, are criteria to distinguish incitement to act from advocacy and debate about the merit of action.

Mill's arguments in chapter two of *On Liberty* have been subject to other criticisms. McCloskey[25] and Acton[26] point out that, contrary to Mill's assertion, all silencing of discussion is *not* an assumption of infallibility. Wolff[27] has claimed that, if an argument from scepticism or ignorance is indeed crucial in *On Liberty*, then Mill's argument has the illiberal implication that 'error has no rights' — that we may be intolerant, providing that we have a rational assurance of the correctness of our beliefs. Though these criticisms may have some force when they are directed against particular remarks in Mill's argument, they neglect a vital aspect of his case. This is that, in the second chapter of *On Liberty* and elsewhere in his writings, Mill acknowledged that different modes of criticism and justification are appropriate in different areas of thought and practice. Further, even in areas such as the natural sciences, where standards of criticism are acknowledged by Mill to be different in character from those pertinent to practical affairs, the account of inquiry given in *On Liberty* is closer to a Popperian[28] error-elimination process or even, it may be, to Feyerabendian[29] pluralism, than it is to the inductivism Mill espouses in the *Logic*. (The connection between Mill's fallibilist theory of knowledge and his political theory will be explored in chapter 6 of this study.) Finally, these traditional criticisms neglect the point, central to Mill's argument, that liberty of thought and expression is valuable, not just instrumentally as a means to the discovery and propagation of truth, but non-instrumentally, as a condition of that rationality and vitality of belief which he conceives of as a characteristic feature of a free man.

Let us consider these points in greater detail. Mill seems to think that, at least in some areas of thought, questions and arguments cannot be fully understood, still less can maxims or principles be adopted, if liberty of discussion is suppressed. As he puts it:[30]

> The fact, however, is that not only the grounds of the opinion are forgotten in the absence of discussion, but too often the meaning of the opinion itself. . . . Instead of a vivid conception and a living belief, there remain only a few phrases retained by rote; or, if any part, the shell and husk only of the meaning is retained, the finer essence lost.

It is tempting to suggest at this point that Mill believes that, in some areas of thought, an element of commitment or at least of imaginative sympathy is necessary if uses of language are even to be understood. His claim then becomes that such commitment or sympathy cannot exist, or at any rate will not typically exist in any very strong form, if the concepts and categories implicit in forms of discourse are not subject to recurrent contestation. In the first part of the claim, Mill may be joining hands with those who think that, with religious language (for example), discourse has an expressive and non-reportive function. In the second part of the claim, he may be suggesting that a form of dialectical reasoning is especially appropriate for some subject-matters, not just as a means to the adoption of well-grounded beliefs, but even as an indispensable condition of understanding. There is here, at least vestigially, a conception of inquiry as being internally related to certain imaginative and emotional as well as intellectual activities. Again, it may well be that Mill is emphasising that the demands of autonomy in thought and practice differ across different areas of thought and forms of life. It would be idle to pretend that any of this is explicit in Mill, however; and it would be dishonest not to admit that some of the things he says in *On Liberty* run counter to these interpretations.

Yet, in a number of places, we find Mill insisting on a distinction between mathematical and other forms of knowledge:[31]

> The peculiarity of the evidence of mathematical truths is that all the argument is on one side. There are no objections. But on every subject in which difference of opinion is possible, the truth depends on a balance to be struck between two sets of conflicting reasons. Even in natural philosophy, there is always some other explanation possible of the same facts . . . and it has to be shown why that other theory cannot be the true one; and until this is shown, and until we know how it is shown, we do not understand the grounds of our opinion.

Mill immediately goes on to make a distinction between different areas of thought, which may be seen as turning on the peculiarity of practical reasoning when contrasted with reasoning in theoretical studies: 'when we turn to subjects infinitely more complicated, to morals, religion, politics, social relations, and to the business of life, three-fourths of the arguments for every opinion consist in dispelling the appearances which favour the opinion different from it.[32]

The salience of the distinction between practical and theoretical reasoning I have suggested is supported by a statement in the same chapter: 'Truth, in the great practical concerns of life, is so much a question of the reconciling and combining of opposites, that very few have minds sufficiently capacious and impartial to make the adjustment with an approach to correctness . . .'.[33] And Mill empha-sises the indispensable utility of the practice of critical discussion in a number of other places:[34]

> He [man] is capable of rectifying his mistakes, by discussion and experience. Not by experience alone. There must be discussion, to show how experience is to be interpreted. Wrong opinions and practices gradually yield to fact and argument; but facts and argu-ments, to produce any effect on the mind, must be brought before it. Very few facts are able to tell their own story, without comments

to bring out their meaning . . . the only way in which a human
being can make some approach to knowing the whole of a subject,
is by hearing what can be said about it by persons of every variety of
opinion, and studying all modes in which it can be looked at by
every character of mind.

Again:[35]

If even the Newtonian philosophy were not permitted to be ques-
tioned, mankind could not feel as complete assurance of its truth as
they do now. The beliefs which we have most warrant for have no
safeguard to rest on, but a standing invitation to the whole world
to prove them unfounded. If the challenge is not accepted, or is
accepted and the attempt fails, we are far enough from certainty
still; what we have done is the best that the existing state of human
reason admits of; we have neglected nothing that could give the
truth a chance of reaching us. If the lists are kept open, we may
hope that if there be a better truth, it will be found when the human
mind is capable of receiving it, and in the meantime we may rely on
having attained such approach to truth as is possible in our own day.
This is the amount of certainty attainable by an fallible being, and
this is the sole way of attaining it.

Yet again:[36]

The Socratic dialectics . . . were essentially a negative discussion of
the great questions of philosophy and life, directed with consum-
mate skill to the purpose of convincing anyone who had merely
adopted the commonplaces of received opinion that he did not
understand the subject – that he as yet attached no definite meaning to the doctrines he professed . . . . It is the fashion of the present
time to disparage negative logic – that which points out weaknesses
in theory or errors in practice, without establishing positive truths.
Such negative criticism would indeed be poor enough as an ultimate
result, but as a means of attaining any positive knowledge or conviction worthy the name, it cannot be valued too highly; and until
people are again systematically trained to it, there will be few great
thinkers, and a low general average of intellect, in any but the
mathematical and physical departments of speculation. On any other
subject no one's opinions deserve the name of knowledge, except so
far as he has either had forced upon him by others, or gone through
of himself, the same mental process which would have been required

Of him in carrying on an active controversy with opponents.

The lack in Mill's writing of any fully adequate treatment of these matters should not induce a hasty dismissal of what he has to say about freedom of expression. As I have interpreted him, he regards freedom of expression as partly constitutive of autonomous agency. Further, the pursuit of truth in at least some areas of inquiry cannot be separated from the practice of critical discussion: truth itself is sometimes regarded by Mill as but the upshot of open debate in these areas. For these reasons, freedom of expression is not to be traded off against anything else, save where this is necessary to forestall moral catastrophe. Though Mill's account may appear to accord to expressive acts a privileged status, this impression is seen to be delusive, once it is realised that these acts come within the vital interest in autonomy which the Principle of Liberty protects.

VI

MILL'S DOCTRINE OF LIBERTY: A REAPPRAISAL

1 THE DOCTRINE OF LIBERTY AND MILL'S GENERAL PHILOSOPHY

If my interpretation has shown anything, it is that Mill's Doctrine of Liberty invokes his view of human nature and applies his conception of happiness. The defining thesis of Mill's indirect utilitarianism — that the direct promotion of happiness is self-defeating — trades on claims about man and society without whose support it is bound to lack credibility. In Humean fashion, Mill takes it for granted that human beings are creatures of limited sympathies and understanding and never doubts that any viable moral code must take full account of these limitations. Taken by itself, however, this side of Mill's indirect utilitarianism in no way supports the priority of liberty. In Hume's case, an indirect utilitarian argument yielded a form of moral and political conservatism in which the claims of liberty have no special or central prominence. In part Mill's difference from Hume is just his belief in the possibility of moral progress, grounded in his almost unlimited confidence in the efficacy of social education and self-cultivation. But Mill's adherence to a doctrine of progress does not by itself show why progress should consist in the promotion of human freedom. For this latter claim, it seems, Mill must draw on claims about human nature other than those acknowledged in the argument for indirect utilitarianism which he has in common with Hume. A major task of the present chapter will be to try to identify these claims, and assess how far they are sustainable.

One of Mill's difficulties is that it is not clear if his view of human nature coheres with his official account of the nature of mind and action. Does the picture of the free society of autonomous men given in *On Liberty* square with the positions in philosophical psychology defended in *A System of Logic*? This question is most commonly asked in the context in which Mill himself chiefly considered it, that of the compatibility of his version of determinism with his concern for individuality and self-cultivation. As is well known, Mill had in common with Hume the view that the causation of human actions was in no way incompatible with the ascription to human beings of powers of self-determination and self-transformation. This compatibilist thesis is as controversial now as it was when Mill revived it. It may be that, in order to sustain it, Mill would need to make a distinction that he never made clearly or explicitly between the knowledge men acquire by observation and experiment on the external world and the reflexive and intentional knowledge they have of their own motives and desires, and then show that regarding man as part of the order of nature and human actions as part of natural causal chains is consistent with ascribing to men the capacity for self-transformation through the acquisition of reflexive knowledge of themselves. That the knowledge gained through participation in experiments in living is such reflexive knowledge is hinted by Mill here and there, but the connections between his compatibilist stance in the philosophy of mind and his account of self-cultivation and of undertaking experiments in living are nowhere clearly brought out by him. If I am right in thinking that it has not been shown conclusively that a naturalistic and deterministic view of man renders impossible the ascription to men of the power of reflexive thought by the exercise of which they alter and improve themselves, then Mill's distinctively political theory has not in this respect been shown to be undermined by his official account of mind and action. Certainly it cannot simply be assumed that there is an inconsistency here.

Another question concerns whether Mill's moral and political theory is consistent with his account of personal identity. In his *Examination of Sir William Hamilton's Philosophy* Mill eventually abandoned the attempt to develop a Humean dissolutionist account of personal self-identity, not in favour of a holistic account, however, but rather from a conviction of the intractableness of the whole problem. The important point is that a complex or no-ownership account of the self is forced on Mill by his general commitment to an empiricist metaphysic. For an empiricist, surely, what matters[1] in the individuation of persons, finally, must be bodily and mental continuity, which unlike strict identity, is a matter of degree. But, if the complex view of personal identity is true, there will be at least some cases where the distinction between self-regarding and other-regarding areas loses force *even within a single life.* We have interpreted Mill's account of the self-regarding area as being framed by the protected vital interests which ground a man's moral rights, but, where continuities are suffic-iently attenuated, we may need to individuate two or more persons within a single lifetime. This is a procedure whose bearing on liberal utilitarian proscriptions of paternalism has already been mentioned. It might be thought that any principles conferring strong moral rights on individuals — rights capable, that is to say, of being invoked against many of the claims of collective welfare — involve insisting on what Rawls and Nozick have each characterised as the moral importance of the separateness of individual selves.[2] If the complex theory of personal identity is true, however, it is hard to see how any such moral distinctions can find a foothold. This is so difficult an area of inquiry that I do not want to pronounce dogmatically on the questions it generates. It does not seem at all obvious, though, that Mill's theory of justice and the moral rights is as seriously threatened by the truth of the complex thesis as, say, Nozick's might be. Strong theories of moral rights may have specific metaphysical presuppositions, but it has yet to be shown that they are committed to a holistic view of the self.

A different range of questions concerns the relations between Mill's view of morality and his account of scientific knowledge. In this connection it cannot be denied that there are large lacunae in Mill's theory of morality. In his 'proof' of utility he seems to stand between those (moral cognitivists) who think that there can be knowledge of moral and practical values and principles and those for whom the adoption of such principles is primarily a matter of sentiment or com-mitment. Similarly, it is hard to pin down Mill's position in the theory of intrinsic value. At times he seems to follow his utilitarian forebears in thinking that only states of mind and feeling can have value for their own sake, but on other occasions he seems to want to allow that activities, relationships and states of affairs can have a value indepen-dent of their contribution to any state of mind so long as they satisfy the preferences of autonomous men. He stands between mental-state utilitarianism and modern preference-utilitarianism. That there are these loose ends in Mill's theory of morality can hardly be denied, but I cannot see that they injure fatally his view of morality as capable of rational assessment and progressive development. The unclarities I have mentioned in Mill's moral epistemology and his theory of intrinsic value do not show his account of moral precepts as depending on scientific theorems to be unsound. Mill's view is not that moral precepts are justified by reference to scientific laws, but that any moral precept will depend on assumptions or conjectures about the ends which adopting it will serve. On Mill's view, morality will be revised as scientific knowledge grows. Mill's crucial assumption here is that morality, like practical reasoning in general, is teleological in structure. This belief is not impugned by the doubts I have mentioned about moral realism and intrinsic value, though it will be weakened if, as has been powerfully argued in Robert Nozick's *Philosophical Explanations*,[3] moral reasoning cannot be analysed as if it possesses a simple structure of any sort.

Moral life can have a progressive aspect, on Mill's account of it, only if scientific knowledge in general, and knowledge in psychology and sociology in particular, itself makes progress. Mill's defence of induction in the theory of scientific knowledge, and his attempt to apply the inductivist programme in the social sciences, aim to validate this sort of growth in knowledge. I have noted already, however, an embarrassing gap in Mill's inductivist reconstruction of the social sciences, his failure to produce even a single law of ethology or character formation. This gap is embarrassing for Mill not just because it leaves his reconstruction of social science incomplete, but because it poses a threat to the scientific credentials of the Doctrine of Liberty. It was Mill's hope, after all, that the psychological claims on which the doctrine rests could be established scientifically, and not simply be reasonable inferences from common sense. Without this scientific basis in sociology and psychology, the doctrine seems to be left hanging in mid air. I will return to this point in the next section of this chapter, when I consider if the doctrine can be detached from Mill's liberalism, with its questionable and implausible claims about the irreversibility of the condition of freedom.

Even if the gap in Mill's science of ethology were filled, another problem stands out for the consistency of the argument of *On Liberty* with Mill's theory of knowledge. Some writers, among whom Paul Feyerabend is the most interesting and eloquent example, have claimed that the theory of knowledge presupposed by *On Liberty* is different from that defended in *A System of Logic*. Thus Feyerabend claims that *On Liberty* advocates a pluralistic methodology in which the importance of many different and conflicting theories, and many rival approaches to understanding of the world, is defended. At one point Feyerabend goes so far as to praise Mill for commendable inconsistency in dropping his official theory of knowledge (in which the unity of scientific method is asserted) in *On Liberty*. Feyerabend's interpretation identifies a real dilemma for Mill. Mill seems to be in a dilemma if knowledge is indeed so reliably cumulative as he hoped and the practice of science converges on a single body of theory. Mill believed diversity of theoretical commitments as well as of forms of life to be a necessary condition of progress, but this diversity will be threatened if the unification of science is a real possibility. That Mill was aware of this difficulty is shown by his proposal for the institution of a devil's advocate in those areas where the progress of knowledge has diminished or eliminated diversity of outlook, but his proposal hardly meets the difficulty. We can go some distance towards meeting it if we take note of the distinction, made by Mill but not systematically developed by him, between criticism and justification in science and in practical life. If, as Mill says in *On Liberty*, practical questions do not allow for the kind of resolution possible in science, then it may be that convergence on any single outlook is far less likely in moral and political life. This would restrict the persuasive force that the argument of *On Liberty* could expect to have, but it would preserve one of the conditions of moral and intellectual progress. Again, Feyerabend has himself elsewhere noted — and in this he is, so far as I know, alone among Mill's interpreters — that the arguments for pluralism and unfettered experimentation in styles of life given in *On Liberty* have their counterparts in *A System of Logic* where the crucial importance for the growth of knowledge and the practice of science of having many alternative theories at one's disposal is emphatically stated. As Feyerabend puts it:[5]

> Interestingly enough, elements of the principle [of proliferation] are found even in Mill's *Logic*. According to Mill, hypotheses, i.e. suppositions 'we make (either without actual evidence, or on evidence avowedly insufficient)' and for which 'there are no other limits . . . than those of the human imagination; we may, if we please, imagine, by way of accounting for an effect, some cause of a kind utterly unknown, and acting in accordance to a law altogether fictitious' — such hypotheses 'are absolutely indispensable in science'.

Feyerabend's observations suggest that the gap between Mill's 'official' philosophy of science and that arguably presupposed by

On Liberty may be far narrower than is ordinarily imagined. So far as I can see, arguments for an incompatibility between Mill's moral and political theory and his official account of knowledge, mind, action and personal identity, are at best inconclusive. Even if they could be shown to be sound, it is not clear that the Doctrine of Liberty would be undermined. The most I have claimed about *On Liberty* is that the conception of a free man that it endorses is consonant with some aspects of Mill's philosophical psychology, not that Mill's arguments for liberty in any way depend upon the positions he adopts as to these other questions. The Doctrine of Liberty would be worth examining, and could have a claim on reason, even if the whole of Mill's larger philosophy were rejected. At the same time, there can be no doubt that Mill saw the argument of *On Liberty* as continuous with his project for a progressive theory of morality in which a revisable moral code is grounded in corrigible scientific theory. But as I have already had occasion to observe, Mill did not in fact give the Doctrine of Liberty that foundation in scientific knowledge he wished for it. The question remains if this conclusion can now be rectified and, if not, whether it matters.

2 THE DOCTRINE OF LIBERTY AND THE SCIENCE OF SOCIETY

As I have expounded it, Mill's Doctrine of Liberty comprises three main principles: first, the Principle of Utility together with its corollary, Expediency: second, the Principle of Liberty; and, third, supplementing the other two, an unstated Principle of Equity, which (like the Principle of Liberty) Mill thinks distinct from Utility but derivable from it. There are three kinds of arguments that Mill advances in support of the adoption of the Principle of Liberty. First, he invokes certain truisms about man and society to show that direct utilitarianism has a self-defeating effect which constrains us to adopt indirect and oblique strategies for the promotion of welfare. Next Mill identifies certain vital interests — the interests in autonomy and security — and contends that no principle can govern the terms of social co-operation unless, like the Principle of Liberty, it protects these vital interests. Whereas Mill's first argument is that the good utilitarian needs a principle distinct from Utility itself for practical conduct, this second argument specifies the principle as part of a theory of justice concerned to ground moral rights as the protection of vital interests. Third, Mill makes certain historical and psychological claims, aiming to support the general priority of autonomy over security in the vital interests and their associated moral rights. Of these arguments, it is the third set that depends most obviously and most crucially on the content of social scientific theory. But is it true that Mill's argument fails because he does not himself provide the needed social theory?

Mill's argument will not fail if we are in a better position than Mill to supply the needed theory. In fact, however, we are in little better a position to do so than Mill himself. The laws of formation of character are not much understood in our own day — notwithstanding decades of psychoanalytic speculation and the investigations of social psychology — and we have no alternative to falling back on casual empiricism and common sense for evidence with which to assess Mill's view of man. It is to enlightened common sense, and to the verdict of undeceived introspection, that Mill himself most often appeals in his efforts to show that the full human valuation of freedom is underestimated in moral theory. Thus in *The Subjection of Women* he declares that:[6]

> He who would rightly appreciate the worth of personal indepen-
> dence as an element of happiness should consider the value he him-
> self puts on it as an ingredient of his own. There is no subject on
> which there is a greater habitual difference of judgement between a
> man judging for himself, and the same man judging for other people.
> When he hears others complaining that they are not allowed freedom
> of action — that their own will has not sufficient influence in the
> regulation of their affairs — his inclination is, to ask, what are their
> grievances? What positive damage do they sustain? And in what
> respect they consider their affairs to be mismanaged? And if they
> fail to make out, in answer to these questions, what appears to him
> a sufficient case, he turns a deaf ear, and regards their complaint
> as the fanciful querulousness of people whom nothing reasonable
> will satisfy. But he has quite a different standard of judgement when
> he is deciding for himself.

We see here Mill's most typical kind of argument for the value of liberty as an ingredient of happiness. It is an argument in which a plea for psychological realism is conjoined with an appeal to moral imagination. It is argued that we tend to take for granted in our own case something — the importance of independence and self-directed activity in sustaining a sense of self-worth that is essential to well-being — which we habitually neglect in considering the lives of others. This is not the sort of argument for which a foundation in scientific social psychology is given or needed, but it is entirely typical of Mill's writings. It is the dominance of this commonsensical approach in Mill's argument for liberty that is missed by those such as Cowling[7] who are over-impressed by Mill's connections with Positivism and who tend to understate his sharp criticism of some of the main tenets of Positivism. My point here is that, whereas Mill never abandoned the project of a science of society linked by a unity of method with the science of nature, and while the Doctrine of Liberty must remain incomplete from his own standpoint so long as it has not been grounded (along with the rest of the Art of Life) in scientific knowledge, none the less, Mill provides telling arguments from common sense and ordinary experience for the picture of human psychology on which the doctrine rests. The arguments he gives are straightforward moral arguments, and are to be assessed as such. Since neither Mill nor his critics have knowledge of the sort which would enable a decisive verdict to be reached, the assessment of the psychological postulates of his doctrine must be a matter of reasonable opinion. At the very least, it has not been shown that Mill's opinion of the ordinary moral psychology of the men with whom *On Liberty* is concerned is definitely unreasonable.

I have not claimed more for Mill than that his argument shows a commitment to liberty to be in utilitarian terms a reasonable wager. It may still be suspected that Mill would himself have been unhappy with so modest a result, and I do not want to try to resist this imputation. Mill never relinquished the hope that his loose and informal arguments for liberty would be superseded and replaced by arguments drawn from the science of human nature. Such arguments could never have deductive rigour, given Mill's distinction between art and science and his view of science itself as throughout inductive, and it is unclear how he would have responded to a build-up of counter-evidence about the relations between personal independence and well-being. (How would he have taken Durkheim's speculative inquiries into anomie, for example?) Perhaps he would have insisted on the fallibility of all such researches and tried to draw a liberal moral from this fallibilist premise. Perhaps, in the end, he would try to link up his Aristotelian conception of human happiness with a more Aristotelian conception of essential human nature — though such a move would conflict with all his empiricist commitments. None of these manoeuvres is necessary to us, if we are more modest than Mill could himself have been, and are prepared to sever the Doctrine of Liberty from the project of a unified science of human nature. But does such a disseveration fatally weaken the Doctrine of Liberty by detaching it from Mill's liberalism itself? Let us see.

3 THE DOCTRINE OF LIBERTY AND MILL'S LIBERALISM

If anyone has ever been a true liberal, it was John Stuart Mill, but defining his liberalism is not easy, for all that. There is no broad agreement among social philosophers as to the defining features of liberalism, which we can use as a benchmark for Mill's liberal commitment. On any sensible understanding, however, Mill is a paradigmatic liberal. If, following Dworkin and Ackerman,[8] we call liberal any social philosophy which aims to defend and occupy a point of moral neutrality between rival conceptions of the good life, then Mill is indeed a liberal: so much is clear if, as I have throughout claimed, he never abandoned or seriously compromised the want-regarding character of classical utilitarianism. For utilitarianism in its want-regarding forms is bound to treat all forms of life equally, no matter what conception of the good life they express, so long as their want-regarding content is the same. And this aspect of utilitarianism is preserved in Mill's doctrine, in which a restrictive conception of harm and a revised view of happiness are commended on the ground that their adoption will maximally serve the cause of want-satisfaction.

By reference to the fashionable and, I believe, appropriate test of a commitment to this sort of moral neutrality, Mill emerges as an unqualified liberal. Mill held also to another belief, no less definitive of liberalism, but far less clearly associated with the Doctrine of Liberty. This is a belief in the practical irreversibility of the condition of freedom — a belief which, in Mill's case as in that of the other liberals, was linked with an historically optimistic doctrine of progress. This is to say that, in common with the French Positivists as well as most of the English Utilitarians, Mill saw human history as a whole evincing an inherent tendency (though not, perhaps, an inexorable law) to moral and intellectual progress. Unlike the French Positivists and some at least of his utilitarian ancestry, however, Mill never envisaged further progress as involving any curtailment of the liberal freedoms he argued

119

for in his own day. In this respect, too, then, Mill was an unblemished liberal, but it is this conviction of the inherently progressive character of man and history that is hardest to give any rational credibility. It is not clear why the condition of freedom should have the aspect of irreversibility Mill atributed to it. That men accustomed to making their own choices will prefer to go on making them for themselves can only be for Mill an inductive wager, grounded in social-psychological conjecture. It could attain the status of an apodictic certainty only if Mill were ready to forswear empiricism and nail his colours to the mast of an essentialist definition of man. It may well be that this latter move is his only recourse if his conviction of the inherent progressive character of human history and his belief in the irreversibility of the condition of liberty are to be sustained.

For Mill, there can be no doubt that the Doctrine of Liberty was bound up with the larger claims of his liberalism. I suggest we adopt a strategy of argument more consistently empiricist that Mill's if we treat the commitment to liberty as grounded in an inductive wager about the future of human nature. If we do this, we will be sacrificing the moral certainty that Mill's liberal beliefs afforded him, but to which he had no right in the empiricist terms of his general philosophy. At the same time we will make of the Doctrine of Liberty a more straight-forwardly empirical argument. It will depend on certain social and psychological conditions and hold good only in cultural milieux where these conditions are satisfied. We will be going one step further than Mill, who allowed that the Doctrine of Liberty applied only when a definite stage of civilisation had been achieved, by acknowledging (as Mill rarely did) that we have no assurance that civilisation can always be maintained. Barbarism remains a permanent possibility, and where the social and moral psychology of barbarism prevails, the conditions demanded by the Doctrine of Liberty are no longer met. It seems to me that severing the Doctrine of Liberty in this way from the larger claims of Mill's liberalism is an unavoidable strategy for anyone unwilling to have recourse to the desperate essentialist expedient of simply defining human flourishing as bounded by the condition of freedom. For if this latter course were adopted, Mill's argument would indeed cease to be a utilitarian one in which only the claims of want-satisfaction are considered.

One way of stating the result of my discussion is to say that the possibilities of conflict between the various levels of Mill's hierarchical utilitarianism, which Mill was able to circumvent only by invoking an implausible theory of progress, must be acknowledged openly. Possibilities of conflict between these levels cannot be excluded, because there can be reasonable differences among men about the powers and prospects of human beings and because on Mill's own account of it human nature as we know it is not fixed or finished. How, then, may these conflicts break out? At the end of the last section of chapter 2 I claimed that Mill's utilitarianism could best be understood if we treated it as a three-tiered theory, applying successively to all sentient creatures, to all men and to men capable of autonomous choice. Later, at the end of the first section of chapter 3, I mentioned the account of the indispensable conditions of social stability given by Mill in the *Logic*. It is these conditions of social stability — involving a system of education and discipline which restrains men's selfish and antisocial passions, a sense of loyalty to basic principles and institutions and a sentiment of commonality or community of interests[9] — which in part motivate Mill's repudiation of any form of direct utilitarianism. They clearly shape the application of utilitarian morality at the second level (as I have called it) of Mill's hierarchical theory, taking account of important general facts about man and entering into Mill's account of the terms of social co-operation. The possibility of conflict arises when it is suggested that applying the requirements of the third level — that is to say, protecting liberty and favouring autonomy as an ingredient of happiness — might subvert the social stability guaranteed at the second level. Another way of stating this same point is to suggest that the third level is never in fact reached. Wollheim, whose hierarchical interpretation of Mill's utilitarianism shares many features with mine, refers obliquely to a similar sort of conflict when he says that 'when the injunctions of preliminary utilitarianism conflict with the injunctions of either simple or complex utilitarianism — whichever is relevant — then, unless the cost in utility is too severe, the injunctions of preliminary utilitarianism take priority'.[10] Wollheim's account of Mill's theory differs from mine in that Wollheim's preliminary utilitarianism has to do with inculcating capacities necessary to the enjoyment of higher pleasures, while simple and complex utilitarianism give different accounts, instrumental and partly constitutive respectively, of the relationship between the pursuit of happiness and observance of secondary maxims. The objection that there may be conflicts between the various levels of the theory applies, however, to Wollheim's account as much as it does to mine. For Mill, Wollheim tells us, 'Education up to the point where happiness can be attained is more important than the attainment either of pleasure or of happiness.'[11] But how does Mill's utilitarianism fare if the cost in utility of preliminary utilitarianism is in fact severe?

The conservative objection to the argument of *On Liberty* has always been that the utility cost of liberal society is indeed 'too severe'. This is the objection of James Fitzjames Stephen, and it is the argument, couched in a more imaginative and uncompromising form, of the Grand Inquisitor in Dostoyevsky's *Brothers Karamazov*. If such criticisms were definitely sound, then the Doctrine of Liberty would assuredly be gravely weakened. Utilitarianism would then be forced back to the doctrines of Bentham and Austin, in which a utilitarian theory of moral rights may certainly be found, but one in which security rather than liberty enjoys primacy. In this case, a breach will have opened up between the author of *On Liberty* and his predecessors and (contrary to the revisionary view incorporated in this study) the continuity of the utilitarian tradition broken. Mill would again be seen as a thinker who seeks refuge from the authoritarian implication of utilitarian ethics by invoking a largely aprioristic and implausible view of human nature. I have already argued that we lack the evidence to assess Mill's view of human nature scientifically. Certainly it cannot yet be said that the evidence goes unequivocally against Mill, or that it clearly favours his conservative critics. Most likely, Mill was over-optimistic, and the societies in which the third tier of his utilitarian theory comes into play are far rarer than he supposed. If this is so, his doctrine is still not overthrown, but only given a more restricted application. The commitment to liberty which the third tier of his theory embodies in respect of the future of mankind in general, however, can only have the character of a wager. It is not a commitment forced on a utilitarian by incontestable evidence, and it does not have the support of contingent but unalterable general facts about man and society possessed by the first and the second tier of the theory. The cardinal error of Mill's conservative critics is to overlook the theoretical and indirect character of Mill's utilitarian theory of the Art of Life, and to make the unwarranted and dogmatic claim that available evidence tells decisively against the psychological and historical claims made in its third tier. My argument is that the commitment to the priority of liberty may be reasonable even if (as is manifestly the case) the evidence we have at our disposal is not such as to force any policy on us as the only one justifiable in utilitarian terms.

The disadvantage of my interpretation is that, in detaching the

Doctrine of Liberty from the larger claims of Mill's liberalism, it allows the doctrine to support only a wager on liberty. A dissever-ation of *On Liberty* from the larger issues of Mill's liberalism does, however, have some corresponding advantages. The Doctrine of Liberty is weakened, in my view, if it has to depend on Mill's Comtist view of the progressive stages of human society, or on his claims for utilitarianism as a religion of humanity. In addition, inter-preting Mill's doctrine in the manner I have suggested enables us to grasp more firmly an important distinction which he himself made. I refer to the distinction between a theory of the rightful limitation of liberty and an account of the proper functions of the state. For Mill, the tasks of the state, apart from its role in enforcing the Principle of Liberty and the supplementary precept about equity, are never more than a matter of ordinary expediency, of 'time, place and circum-stance', not deducible from any very general principles. Of course, Mill favoured as a general policy the non-interference of the state in social life, but he allowed many exceptions to this policy, and he was explicit in his view that, when the state's activity is 'non-authoritative' — that is to say, when it involves no coercion or restriction of liberty beyond that incurred in the levying and deploying of tax revenues — it cannot be delimited in detail or once for all. We find in Mill's own writings, then, a recognition that the principle of non-interference, though supported by many of the same considerations, is different in kind from the Principle of Liberty. The latter specifies a constraint on the state's activities to which it must conform, once the required level of civilisation has been reached, whereas the non-interference principle merely states a weighty presumption against the expansion of state activity. When he discusses the extent of state activity in the last chapter of *On Liberty*, it is quite clear that, though they flow from similar concerns, Mill's opinions on this question are intended to weigh with us as general considerations and not as rigid constraints on political life. He puts the matter himself with exemplary clarity in the last chapter of *On Liberty*. There he says: 'The objections to government interference, when it is not such as to involve infringe-ment of liberty, may be of three kinds.' He goes on, in expanding upon the third of these reasons against government interference, to assert:[12]

If the roads, the railways, the banks, the insurance offices, the great joint-stock companies, the universities, and the public charities, were all of them branches of the government; if, in addition, the municipal corporations and local boards, with all that now devolves on them, become departments of the central administration; if the employees of all these different enterprises were appointed and paid by the government, and looked to the government for every rise in life; not all the freedom of the press and popular constitution of the legislature would make this or any other country free otherwise than in name.

Here Mill's argument is that an expansion of government interference in social life, while 'not such as to involve infringement of liberty', may effectively stifle liberty when it is carried beyond a certain real, if necessarily imprecise point.

A crucial implication of this distinction between the Doctrine of Liberty and the theory of the proper sphere of state activity is that the doctrine is silent on the question of socialism. One who accepted the doctrine may, as Mill did himself, favour some kinds of socialist experimentation. Certainly, Mill did not see existing property rights as erecting any insuperable barrier to such experimentation, though his preference was that it be highly voluntaristic.[13] On the other hand, someone with a different reading of the available evidence might adopt a much more restrictive view of the state's proper functions, and even see them as exhausted by the enforcement of the Principle or Liberty. It is the cardinal error of Mill's libertarian critics[14] that, in neglecting Mill's own distinction between the rightful limitations of liberty and the question of the limits of state interference, they omit to notice this last possibility. Again, nothing in the Doctrine of Liberty prevents the state from going beyond the task of harm-prevention and seeking to benefit its citizens or men in general, providing such welfarist activities involve no coercive or 'authoritative' limitations on liberty. The important point is that there is nothing inexorable about any of these moves. Mill's Principle of Liberty does not exclude the possibility of his favouring socialism any more than his utilitarian commitment binds him to support welfarist policies.

The principle of state non-interference in social affairs is thus an independent and distinct principle, not the Principle of Liberty or any part of Mill's Doctrine of Liberty. It is supported, I have conceded, by many of the same utilitarian considerations which ground the Principle of Liberty, but it is treated by Mill quite differently, as a fallible rule of thumb, derivable from utility but not justifiably treated as framing a (utility-maximising) constraint on the direct pursuit of utility. Mill's

124

views on the limits of state interference are to be assessed in the spirit in which they were advanced, as proposals appropriate to the circumstances of his time. But my point is not to settle the very large question of whether Mill's views on the functions of the state were reasonable, in his terms or ours, but merely to remark that objections to his views in these areas are not criticisms of his Doctrine of Liberty.

4 THE UTILITY OF THE DOCTRINE OF LIBERTY

As I have interpreted it, the Doctrine of Liberty shows a commitment to liberty, as embodied in a system of moral rights, to be defensible in utilitarian terms. If I have shown this modest claim to be beyond reasonable doubt, I have overturned the central claim of traditional Mill criticism — that the project Mill undertook in *On Liberty* in founding a utilitarian right to liberty expresses a conceptual and a moral impossibility. It remains to confront a different criticism of Mill — that his Doctrine of Liberty fails to afford the sort of guidance to practical life Mill expected of it.

The objection I have in mind is put in radical and succinct form by Alasdair Macintyre in his recent important study *After Virtue*. Macintyre observes:

> John Stuart Mill was right of course in his contention that the Benthamite conception of happiness stood in need of enlargment; in *Utilitarianism* he attempted to make a key distinction between 'higher' and 'lower' pleasures and in *On Liberty* and elsewhere he connects increase in human happiness with the extension of human creative powers. But the effect of these emendations is to suggest — what is correct, but what no Benthamite no matter how reformed could concede — that the notion of human happiness is not a unitary, simple notion and cannot provide us with a criterion for making our key choices.

Macintyre concludes: 'To have understood the polymorphous character of pleasure and happiness is of course to have rendered those concepts useless for utilitarian purposes.'[15] I trust that the arguments of the previous chapters show Macintyre's claim to be exaggerated. The abstractness and complexity of Mill's conception of happiness represents the attempt in a spirit of psychological realism to come to grips with the diversity and variety of human purposes and to identify happiness with the successful pursuit of self-chosen goals rather than with the having of any sort of sensation. Again, the theory of vital interests aims to identify fundamental and constitutive elements in human happiness and to give utilitarian reason why these should be ranked over the rest. Macintyre's claims assume, but do not establish, that Mill's attempt to marry utilitarian ethics to a more realistic and complex psychology was bound to prove abortive. But why should it?

This is not to say that Mill's conception of happiness in fact contains the elements needed to settle basic practical dilemmas. Consider the pair of vital interests. No doubt they are not altogether separable, since the secure protection of the interest in autonomy is part of protecting autonomy itself and the protection of the interest in security must include guaranteeing a sphere of freedom of action from arbitrary invasion. Autonomy and security remain distinct interests even if they are not altogether separable, however, and different policies will affect them differently. When policies affect these interests differently, we might still reasonably disagree as to which of them is to be favoured when they compete. Mill, it is true, thought autonomy ought always to be given the benefit of the doubt, but he did not hold that autonomy must be ranked lexically over security as the pair of vital interests is over all other interests. Even for Mill, then, the problem remains. Perhaps it is Mill's supposition that, as with the higher pleasures, the judgment of autonomous experienced men will converge within a fairly limited range of answers to practical questions. Certainly, there is a pragmatic turn in Mill's moral and political thought which might issue in such a proposal. In this case, applying the liberty principle to questions of intervention would itself presuppose appeal to the decision-procedure Mill invokes to support his theory of the highest pleasures. As I have noted, however, that decision-procedure fails when it comes up against conflicts among the elements of an agent's own happiness. It cannot be gainsaid that Mill's doctrine does not cope with these ultimate conflicts of value or with the practical dilemmas they generate. To this extent, those who have tried to square a version of value-pluralism with Mill's utilitarianism − as Wollheim does in his response to Berlin's criticism of Mill[16] − do not confront the problem of the incompatibility of some of the elements of happiness. This point is tacitly conceded by Wollheim himself, when in his suggestive Leslie Stephen Lecture *The Sheep and the Ceremony* he admits that:[17]

within this sphere [of preliminary utilitarianism] no mechanical method for arriving at clear answers exists. If we had well-confirmed laws governing the development of human character, or what Mill called a science of 'ethology', answers might be readily forthcoming. In their absence such issues must be settled by trial and error, where the criteria of error are essentially contestable and the trial involves evidence far more ramified than straightforward or ineligible Utilitarianism would consider admissible.

Inasmuch as it is silent on this question, Mill's doctrine fails to give the practical advice Mill asked and expected of it. It remains unclear what Utility demands because it is unclear how we are to weigh its competing elements. For a value-pluralist, indeed, such a weighting of incommensurables is an impossibility. There must be this divergence between utilitarianism and value-pluralism if the two doctrines are to be distinguishable. Mill's theory remains a utilitarian theory, distinguishable from value-pluralism, if only because of the crucial claim Mill defends in utilitarian terms that the vital interests are in the circumstances with which he is concerned always to be ranked over men's other interests. For this reason alone, Mill's utilitarianism does not suffer the fate invoked by Bernard Williams against some other forms of indirect utilitarianism, that in order to be effective it must leave no distinctive mark in the world.[18]

Mill's theory cannot deliver us from the necessity of making uncomfortable choices between the various elements of happiness. Nor can it be insulated from the threat posed to the claims of liberty by a large-scale mutation in men's interests and characters. This follows inexorably, if we withdraw from the doctrine the dubious support that might be claimed for it from Mill's theory of human progress.[19] It might still be thought that, even given these qualifications, I have claimed too much for the doctrine. After all, Mill himself has told us that 'If I am asked, what system of political philosophy I substituted for that which, as a philosophy, I had abandoned (after the Mental Crisis), I answer, no system: only a conviction that the true system was something much more complex and many-sided than I had previously had any idea of.'[20] Does not Mill here disavow anything as definite even as the Doctrine of Liberty I ascribe to him? I think not. Mill's abandonment of the crudities of Benthamite psychology and philosophy of politics, and his adoption of a theory of progress as the central principle of his moral and political thought, do not affect my claim that his writings contain a systematic theory of liberty of which *On Liberty* itself is but the most important fragment. The theory of the Art of Life, as set out in the *Logic*, with its distinction beteen critical and practical levels of thought about all the departments of human life and its advocacy of an evalua- tive rather than a prescriptive utilitarianism, is linked explicitly with the arguments of *Utilitarianism*, and these in turn are connected by many clear links of intelligibility with the arguments of *On Liberty*. To develop a doctrine about liberty was avowedly Mill's intention in *On Liberty*. If the real limitation of his enterprise there is that it exaggerates the practical force of doctrinal political theory, that does not mean there is no doctrine there to be appraised, any more than his disavowal of any overall system in philosophy means that he was an unsystematic thinker. The fact remains that, whether or not Mill made this demand of it, his doctrine cannot supply a mechanical rule for the resolution of all important questions about the limitation of liberty.

This fundamental limitation of Mill's theory does not, however, altogether deprive it of practical utility. It shows up an area of practical and moral conflict which Mill's theory cannot give complete guidance in resolving – but this is not to say that the theory is silent in the face of such conflicts, or that it says nothing of the contexts in which they occur. The crucial claim of the doctrine – that there are utilitarian reasons for according the vital interests in autonomy and security a privileged immunity from utilitarian trade-off – is not touched by this criticism. If this crucial claim is supported, then Mill's theory emerges as superior to those liberal doctrines which, in taking the right to liberty along with other rights as axiomatic or self-evident, effectively abandon the search for a justificatory theory for liberty. That the elements of happiness may conflict with one another and are not easily comparable does not overturn the central and most impor- tant claims of Mill's theory, but only restricts its practical, action- guiding force.

Whereas this, the most powerful criticism of Mill's doctrine, res- tricts its utility and disappoints some of Mill's hopes for it, the limit- ation it points to in the doctrine is not peculiar to it. It is a feature of all social philosophy that it breaks off at the point at which we need to resolve ultimate dilemmas in practical life. Strictly, then, the criticism is not of Mill's doctrine so much as of any social philosophy which neglects the underdetermination of moral and political life by theory. Further, this ultimate limitation of the doctrine by no means deprives it of practical force or contemporary interest. In disallowing a vast range of considerations — welfarist, paternalist and moralist, to mention only a few — as sufficient to justify imposing limits on liberty, the doctrine still retains controversial vitality. In proposing a hierarchical utilitarian account of which reasons are to be disqualified as salient to liberty-limiting policy, the doctrine invites criticism as a challenging application of a neglected species of utilitarianism. The doctrine retains practical utility and philosophical interest, even if it fails to live up to all of Mill's hopes for it.

The scope of the doctrine, then, may be narrower than Mill thought, and the power of the doctrine to cope with practical dilemmas less than he hoped. Its distinctive virtue, though, remains what it always was. It is an attempt to show to those who care little for liberty what are its benefits. As long as there are among Mill's readers those who have known the advantages of liberty, or whose character and circumstances intimate a value for liberty which they have not so far acknowledged, *On Liberty* will remain worth reading. Indeed, *On Liberty* will remain a cogent argument in support of liberal principles, even if the social order it defends is rare, difficult to achieve and impossible to sustain for long.

NOTES

I MILL'S PROBLEM IN *ON LIBERTY*

1 J. S. Mill, *Utilitarianism, On Liberty and Considerations on Representative Government*, London, Dent, 1972, p. 72.
2 *Ibid.*, p. 73.
3 *Ibid.*, p. 74.
4 *Ibid.*, p. 6.
5 *Ibid.*, pp. 72–3.
6 *Ibid.*, p. 73.
7 *Ibid.*, p. 74.
8 Barry's arguments about the self-defeating effect of liberal principles, which draw on the distinction between want-regarding and ideal-regarding considerations which he made in *Political Argument*, London, Routledge & Kegan Paul, 1965, pp. 41–2, may be found summarised on pp. 126–7 of his *The Liberal Theory of Justice*, Oxford, Clarendon Press, 1973.
9 That liberalism is neutral with respect to competing views of the good life is claimed by Dworkin, most explicitly in his paper 'Liberalism', in *Public and Private Morality*, ed. S. Hampshire, Cambridge University Press, 1978.
10 The view of Mill as a moral totalitarian is developed in Maurice Cowling's *Mill and Liberalism*, Cambridge University Press, 1963, and in S. R. Letwin's *The Pursuit of Certainty*, Cambridge University Press, 1965. The view that, if Mill endorses a specific ideal of human excellence, then he is necessarily implicated in a kind of moral totalitarianism, is very ably criticised by C. L. Ten in his *Mill on Liberty*, Oxford, Clarendon Press, 1980, pp. 146–51.
11 *Ethics*, Oxford University Press, 1966, p. 121.
12 See Ronald Dworkin, *Taking Rights Seriously*, London, Duckworth, 1977, pp. 90–4, 188–92. In the revised edition of his book (1978), Dworkin allows (pp. 294–301, 313–15) that there

may be a consequentialist theory of rights.

13 See Robert Nozick, *Anarchy, State and Utopia*, Oxford, Basil Blackwell, 1974, pp. 28–33.

14 See John Lucas, *On Justice*, Oxford University Press, 1980, ch. 2.

15 See Mill, *op. cit.*, p. 58, footnote.

16 See Fitzjames Stephen, *Liberty, Equality, Fraternity*, Cambridge University Press, 1967.

17 By 'traditional' and 'revisionary' interpretations, I do not intend to refer to two groups of writers, each of which shares a common view on all important points in the interpretation and criticism of Mill on liberty. But important recent statements of a traditional view of Mill on liberty may be found in H. J. McCloskey, *John Stuart Mill: a Critical Study*, London, Macmillan, 1971; and in the writings of Ted Honderich, especially his *Punishment: the Supposed Justifications*, London, Hutchinson, 1969, p. 175 *et seq.*, and his 'The Worth of J. S. Mill on Liberty', *Political Studies*, December 1974, vol. XXII, no. 4, pp. 463–70; and in Isaiah Berlin's 'John Stuart Mill and the Ends of Life', in *Four Essays on Liberty*, Oxford University Press, 1969, p. 173 *et seq.* The revisionary view designates that wave of reinterpretation of Mill begun by Alan Ryan and J. C. Rees in the 1960s. Alan Ryan's main contributions are to be found in 'Mr. McCloskey on Mill's Liberalism', *Philosophical Quarterly*, 1964, vol. 14, pp. 253–60; 'John Stuart Mill's Art of Living', *The Listener*, 22 October 1965, vol. 74, pp. 620–2; *The Philosophy of John Stuart Mill*, London, Macmillan, 1970; *John Stuart Mill*, London, Routledge & Kegan Paul, 1974; 'John Stuart Mill and the Open Society', *The Listener*, 17 May 1973, pp. 633–5. For Rees's contributions, see 'A Rereading of Mill on Liberty', *Political Studies*, 1960, vol. 8, pp. 113–29, reprinted with an important postscript (1965) in P. Radcliff (ed.), *Limits of Liberty*, Belmont, California, 1966, pp. 87–107. Rees's papers 'A Phase in the Development of Mill's Ideas on Liberty', *Political Studies*, 1958, vol. 6, pp. 33–4; 'Was Mill for Liberty?', *Political Studies*, 1966, vol. 14, pp. 72–7; 'The Reaction to Cowling on Mill', *Mill News Letter*, Spring 1966, vol. 1, no. 2, pp. 2–11; and 'The Thesis of the "Two Mills" ', *Political Studies*, 1977, vol. 25, pp. 368–82, should also be consulted, as should his *Mill and his Early Critics*, Leicester University College, 1956. Among other revisionary interpretations, the most notable are those of D. G. Brown, David Lyons and C. L. Ten. See D. G. Brown, 'Mill on Liberty and Morality', *Philosophical Review*, 1972, vol. 81, pp. 133–58. I am indebted also to Brown's papers on 'What is Mill's Principle of Utility?', *Canadian Journal of Philosophy*, 1973, vol. 3, pp. 1–12; 'Mill's Act-Utilitarianism', *Philosophical Quarterly*, 1974, pp. 67–8; 'John Rawls: John Mill', *Dialogue*, 1973, vol. XII, no. 3. I have profited also from Brown's 'Mill on Harm to Others' Interests', *Political Studies*, 1978, vol. XXVI, pp. 395–9. G. L. Williams (see below) has given a short

reply to Brown's 'Mill on Harm to Others' Interests' in *Political Studies*, 1980, vol. XXVIII, pp. 295-6. For the definitive statement of C. L. Ten's view of Mill on liberty, see his excellent book, *Mill on Liberty* (as cited in note 10 above). For David Lyons's contributions, see his 'Mill's Theory of Morality', *Nous*, 1976, vol. 10, pp. 101−20; 'Human Rights and the General Welfare', *Philosophy and Public Affairs*, 1977, vol. 6, pp. 113−29. His recent paper, 'Mill's Theory of Justice', which appears in A. I. Goldman and J. Kim (eds), *Values and Morals*, Dordrecht, D. Reidel, 1978, pp. 1−20, and his 'Mill on Liberty and Harm to Others', *Canadian Journal of Philosophy*, 1979, Supplementary Volume V, pp. 1−19, are also important sources for the revisionary interpretation. Of crucial importance in developing the interpretation of Mill as an indirect utilitarian is Richard Wollheim's 'John Stuart Mill and Isaiah Berlin: The Ends of Life and the Preliminaries of Morality', in Alan Ryan (ed.), *The Idea of Freedom*, Oxford University Press, 1979, pp. 253−69, and Wollheim's *The Sheep and the Ceremony: the Leslie Stephen Lecture, 1979*, Cambridge University Press, pp. 28−33. See also G. L. Williams: 'Mill's Principle of Liberty', *Political Studies*, 1976, vol. XXIV, pp. 13−140, his introduction to his edition of *J. S. Mill on Politics and Society*, London, Fontana, 1976, pp. 41−2, and his reply to Brown (cited above).

I have benefited from R. J. Halliday, 'Some Recent Interpretations of J. S. Mill', in J. B. Schneewind (ed.), *Mill: a collection of critical essays*, London, Macmillan, 1968, pp. 354−78, together with Halliday's book *John Stuart Mill*, London, Allen & Unwin, 1976; Rolf Sartorius, *Individual Conduct and Social Norms*, Encino and Belmont, California, Dickenson, 1975; J. P. Dryer, 'Mill's Utilitarianism' may be found in Mill's *Essays on Ethics, Religion and Society*, ed. J. M. Robson, *Collected Works of John Stuart Mill*, vol. X, Toronto University Press, 1969, pp. lxii−cxiii; Richard B. Friedman, 'A New Exploration of Mill's Essay on Liberty', *Political Studies*, 1966, vol. XIV, pp. 281−304.

I have learnt much from Fred Berger's published and unpublished writings on Mill, the most important of the former being contained in the *Canadian Journal of Philosophy* supplementary volume cited below in this note. D. G. Long's *Bentham on Liberty*, University of Toronto Press, 1977, is an important study of utilitarian thought, whose Appendix on Bentham and J. S. Mill on liberty, pp. 115−18, should especially be consulted.

An extremely valuable source of recent revisionary interpretations is *New Essays on John Stuart Mill and Utilitarianism*, ed. W. E. Cooper, Kai Nielson and S. C. Pattern, *Canadian Journal of Philosophy*, 1979, Supplementary Volume V, in which the papers by David Lyons, J. P. Dryer, David Copp, L. W. Sumner and Fred Berger are particularly noteworthy.

18 L. W. Sumner, 'The Good and the Right', *Canadian Journal of*

Philosophy, 1979, Supplementary Volume V, pp. 102–3.
19 See H. L. A. Hart, *The Concept of Law*, Oxford University Press, 1961, pp. 189–95.
20 The notion of a side-constraint principle I use here is Nozick's, borrowed from *Anarchy, State and Utopia* (see above, note 13), pp. 28–35. Nozick himself denies that any adequate utilitarian account can be given of the moral importance of side-constraints. See Nozick's brilliant *Philosophical Explanations*, Oxford, Clarendon Press, 1981, p. 495.

II MILL'S UTILITARIANISM

1 J. S. Mill, *A System of Logic*, bk VI, ch XII, section 6.
2 *Ibid.*
3 *Ibid.*
4 On this see D. G. Brown, 'What is Mill's Principle of Utility?', *Canadian Journal of Philosophy*, 1973, vol. 3, pp. 1–12.
5 J. S. Mill, *Utilitarianism, On Liberty and Considerations on Representative Government*, London, Everyman, 1972, p. 6.
6 *Ibid.*, p. 11.
7 *Ibid.*, p. 32.
8 *Ibid.*, p. 6.
9 Ted Honderich, 'The Worth of J. S. Mill on Liberty', *Political Studies*, December 1974, vol. XXII, no. 4, p. 467.
10 See H. A. Prichard, 'Does Moral Philosophy Rest on a Mistake?' in Samuel Gorovitz (ed.), *Mill: Utilitarianism*, Indianapolis, Bobbs-Merrill, 1971, p. 63.
11 See David Lyons, 'Mill's Theory of Morality', *Nous*, 1976, vol. 10, pp. 101–20.
12 J. P. Dryer, 'Mill's Utilitarianism' in Mill's *Essays on Ethics, Religion and Society*, ed. J. M. Robson, Collected Works of John Stuart Mill, vol. X, Toronto University Press, 1969, p. lxiv.
13 Mill, *Utilitarianism. . .*, p. 45.
14 The writers I have in mind are D. H. Hodgson, *Consequences of Utilitarianism*, Oxford, Clarendon Press, 1967, and G. J. Warnock, who offers a somewhat different version of the argument that many or most, perhaps all, forms of utilitarianism are self-defeating in *The Object of Morality*, London, Methuen, 1971, pp. 31–4.
15 I refer, especially, to J. O. Urmson's 'The Interpretation of the Moral Philosophy of J. S Mill', *Philosophical Quarterly*, 1954, pp. 33–9.
16 On this see Brown, *op. cit.*
17 Mill, *Utilitarianism. . .*, p. 45.
18 See Urmson's paper, *op. cit.*, collected in J. B. Schneewind's *Mill: a collection of critical essays*, London, Macmillan, 1968, p. 183.
19 See Mill, *Utilitarianism. . .*, p. 55.

20 Urmson, *op. cit.*, Schneewind, pp. 189.
21 J. S. Mill, *Utilitarianism...*, p. 45.
22 J. S. Mill, *Autobiography*, in Max Lerner (ed.), *Essential Works of J. S. Mill*, New York, Bantam Books, 1961, ch. 5, para. 5.
23 J. S. Mill, *Utilitarianism...*, p. 45.
24 C. L. Ten, *Mill on Liberty*, Oxford, Clarendon Press, 1980, p. 48.
25 Rolf Sartorius, *Individual Conduct and Social Norms*, Encino and Belmont, California, Dickenson, 1975, pp. 70–1. For a statement of Hare's version of the thesis, which Ten criticised, but which appeared after Ten's book, see R. M. Hare, *Moral Thinking: its levels, method and point*, Oxford, Clarendon Press, 1981, especially the illuminating questions in ch. 9 of justice and rights in a utilitarian framework.
26 Ten, *op. cit.*, pp. 34–6.
27 *Ibid.*, p. 38.
28 Honderich, *op. cit.*
29 I owe my awareness of the possibilities and difficulties of indirect utilitarianism as a generic doctrine of which J. S. Mill's is only one species to Bernard Williams's discussion of it in chapter 6 of his 'A Critique of Utilitarianism' in J. J. C. Smart and Bernard Williams, *Utilitarianism: for and against*, Cambridge University Press, 1973, pp. 118–35.
30 *A System of Logic*, bk VI, Ch. 12, sect. 6.
31 'Bentham', in G. Himmelfarb (ed.), *J. S. Mill on Politics and Culture*, New York, Doubleday, 1963, p. 116.
32 Mill, *Utilitarianism...*, p. 46. Brown's discussion of Mill's different formulations of the Art of Life occurs in his 'Mill on Liberty and Morality', *Philosophical Review*, 1972, vol. 81, pp. 133–58.
33 R. J. Halliday, *John Stuart Mill*, London, Allen & Unwin, 1976, p. 58.
34 A. Ryan, *John Stuart Mill*, London, Routledge & Kegan Paul, 1974, p. 106.
35 'Bentham', in Himmelfarb (ed.), *op. cit.*, p. 114.
36 On the reception of Mill's 'proof', see Norman Kretzman, 'Desire as proof of desirability', in Gorovitz, *op. cit.*, pp. 231–41.
37 I am most grateful to Professor Berger for letting me read several chapters of his extremely useful book. Berger's account of Mill's conception of happiness has been published in *Interpretation*, 1977, vol. VII, no. 3, under the title 'Mill's Concept of Happiness'.
38 J. S. Mill, *A System of Logic*, bk VI, ch. 2, sect. 4. See also the section on habitual willing in chapter 4 of Utilitarianism, where Mill says: 'Will is the child of desire, and passes out of the dominion of its parent only to come under that of habit' (p. 38, Everyman edn). I am indebted to Dr D. A. Rees for calling my attention to this passage.
39 James Mill, *Analysis of the Phenomena of the Human Mind*, London, 1869, pp. 217–18.
40 J. S. Mill, *Utilitarianism...*, p. 35.

41 *Ibid.*, p. 35.
42 Dryer, *op. cit.*, p. lxviii.
43 *Ibid.*, p. lxxii.
44 Mill, *Utilitarianism.* . ., p. 4.
45 F. E. Mineka and D. N. Lindley (eds), J. S. Mill, *Later Letters*, *Collected Works*, University of Toronto Press, 1972, vol. XVI, p. 1414.
46 J. S. Mill, *Utilitarianism.* . ., p. 115.
47 A perfectionist aspect has been attributed to Mill's utilitarian liberalism by V. Haksar in his *Liberty, Equality and Perfectionism*, Oxford, Clarendon Press, 1979, pp. 230–5, 236–57 *passim*.
48 The term 'want-regarding' is used here in the sense defined in Brian Barry, *Political Argument*, London, Routledge & Kegan Paul, 1965, pp. 38–43.

III THE PRINCIPLE OF LIBERTY

1 J. S. Mill, *Utilitarianism, On Liberty and Considerations on Representative Government*, London, Dent, 1972, p. 72.
2 J. S. Mill, *Autobiography*, in Max Lerner (ed.), *Essential Works of J. S. Mill*, New York, Bantam Books, 1961, p. 149.
3 J. R. Lucas, *Principles of Politics*, Oxford, Clarendon Press, 1966, p. 174.
4 Peter Winch, 'Can a Good Man be Harmed?', in *Ethics and Action*, London, Routledge & Kegan Paul, 1976, pp. 193–209.
5 J. C. Rees, 'A Re-reading of Mill on Liberty', *Political Studies*, 1960, vol. 8, pp. 113–29, reprinted in P. Radcliff (ed.) *Limits of Liberty*, Belmont, California, 1966, pp. 87–107.
6 *Ibid.*, p. 94.
7 I owe this point to Joel Feinberg's 'Harm and Self-Interest' in P. M. S. Hacker and J. Raz (eds), *Law, Morality and Society: Essays in honour of H. L. A. Hart*, Oxford, Clarendon Press, 1977, pp. 285–308.
8 Ress, in Radcliff, *op. cit.*, pp. 101–2.
9 Wollheim, 'J. S. Mill and the Limits of State Action', *Social Research*, Spring 1973, vol. 40, no. 1, pp. 1–30.
10 J. S. Mill, *Utilitarianism.* . ., pp. 55–6, 59–60.
11 Mill recognises emergencies as providing reasons which may justify restricting liberty in *ibid.*, pp. 59–60.
12 See *ibid.*, p. 406.
13 *Ibid.*, p. 50.
14 F. E. Mineka and D. N. Lindley (eds), J. S. Mill, *Later Letters*, University of Toronto Press, 1972, vol. XVII, pp. 1831–2.
15 See H. L. A. Hart, *The Concept of Law*, Oxford, Clarendon Press, 1961, pp. 189–95.
16 Mill, *Utilitarianism.* . ., p. 48.
17 C. L. Ten gives a useful account of the dispute regarding the

force of the Principle of Liberty on pp. 61–7 of his *Mill on Liberty*, Oxford, Clarendon Press, 1980.

18 See A. K. Sen, 'Informational Analysis and Moral Principles', in Ross Harrison (ed.), *Rational Action*, Cambridge University Press, 1979, pp. 115–32.

19 D. G. Brown, 'Mill on Liberty and Morality', *Philosphical Review*, 1972, vol. 81, p. 135.

20 Mill, *Utilitarianism.* . ., pp. 163–4.

21 J. S. Mill, *Principles of Political Economy*, bk V, ch. XI, sects. 1–2.

22 J. S. Mill, *Utilitarianism.* . ., p. 50.

23 This passage is reproduced on p. 309 of G. L. Williams (ed.), *John Stuart Mill on Politics and Society*, London, Fontana, 1976.

24 J. S. Mill, *Utilitarianism.* . ., p. 406.

25 Quoted by D. G. Brown, *Dialogue*, 1973, vol. XII, no. 3, pp. 478–9.

26 R. Nozick, *Anarchy, State and Utopia*, Oxford, Blackwell, 1974, p. 30 (footnote).

27 J. Rawls, *A Theory of Justice*, Oxford University Press, 1972, pp. 62–3.

28 D. H. Regan, *Utilitarianism and Cooperation*, Oxford, Clarendon Press, 1980.

29 The idea of a utilitarianism of rights is suggested by Nozick, *op. cit.*, pp. 28–9.

30 Mill, *Utilitarianism.* . . , p. 132.

31 Mill, *Utilitarianism.* . ., pp. 46–7.

32 On 'public' and 'private' harms, see J. Feinberg, *Social Philosophy*, Englewood Cliffs, New Jersey, Prentice-Hall, 1973, pp. 25–35, 52–4.

IV MILL'S CONCEPTION OF HAPPINESS AND THE THEORY OF INDIVIDUALITY

1 I have discussed negative freedom in my 'On Negative and Positive Freedom', *Political Studies*, December 1980, vol. XXVIII, no. 4, pp. 507–26.

2 See S. I. Benn's 'Freedom, Autonomy and the Concept of a Person', *Proceedings of the Aristotelian Society*, 1976, vol. LXXVI, pp. 109–30.

3 I adopt the terms 'anomic' and 'wanton' from H. G. Frankfurt's discussion in 'Freedom of the Will, and the Concept of a Person', *Journal of Philosophy*, 1971, vol. LXVIII, pp. 5–20.

4 See *ibid.*, pp. 11–12.

5 See David Riesman, *The Lonely Crowd*, New Haven, Yale University Press, 1950, for an elucidation of this idiom.

6 See Frankfurt again, *op. cit.*

7 Joel Feinberg, *Social Philosophy*, Englewood Cliffs, New Jersey, Prentice-Hall, 1973, pp. 15–17.

8 J. S. Mill, *On Liberty, Utilitarianism and Considerations on Representative Government*, London, Dent, 1972, pp. 116–17.
9 *Ibid.*, p. 118.
10 Robert F. Ladenson, 'Mill's Conception of Individuality', *Social Theory and Practice*, 1977, vol. 4, no. 2, pp. 167–82.
11 Mill, *op. cit.*, p. 117.
12 For example, Fred Berger in his important unpublished work on Mill.
13 Robert Paul Wolff, *The Poverty of Liberalism*, Boston, Beacon Press, 1968, p. 19.
14 See, especially, Antony Thorlby, 'Liberty and Self-Development: Goethe and J. S. Mill', *Neohelicon* 1973, vol. 3–4, pp. 91–110.
15 Mill, *op. cit.*, p. 34.
16 *Ibid.*, p. 9.
17 Stuart Hampshire, *Freedom of Mind*, Oxford University Press, 1972, pp. 193–4.
18 Mill, *op. cit.*, p. 128.
19 V. Haksar, *Liberty Equality and Perfectionism*, Oxford University Press, 1978, p. 233.
20 John Finnis, *Natural Law and Natural Rights*, Oxford, Clarendon Press, 1980, pp. 111–18.
21 Brian Barry attributes this view to Rawls and, by implication, J. S. Mill, in his *The Liberal Theory of Justice*, Oxford, Clarendon Press, 1973, p. 28.
22 Rawls discusses his use of the term 'thin theory of the good' in *A Theory of Justice*, Oxford, Oxford University Press, 1972, pp. 395–9.

V APPLICATIONS

1 J. S. Mill, *Utilitarianism, On Liberty and Considerations on Representative Government*, London, Dent, 1972, p. 73.
2 *Ibid.*, pp. 151–2.
3 *Ibid.*, p. 152.
4 J. S. Mill, *Principles of Political Economy*, bk V, ch. XI, sect. 10.
5 Mill, *Utilitarianism. . .*, pp. 157–8.
6 An argument for Mill's consistency on the question of voluntary slavery is given by Vinit Haksar, *Liberty, Equality and Perfectionism*, Oxford University Press, 1979, pp. 250–6, and by J. Hodson, 'Mill, paternalism and slavery', *Analysis*, January 1981, vol. 41, no. 1, pp. 60–2.
7 The commentator I have in mind is D. H. Regan, 'Justifications for Paternalism', in J. R. Pennock and J. W. Chapman (eds), *The Limits of Law*, New York, Lieber-Atherton, 1974, pp. 189–220.
8 The use of Parfit's metaphor of earlier and later selves is discussed by Regan in *ibid.*, pp. 189–220.
9 See J. S. Mill and Harriet Taylor Mill, *Essays on Sex Equality*, ed.

Alice S. Rossi, University of Chicago Press, 1970, pp. 236–40.

10 J. S. Mill, *Utilitarianism. . .*, London, Dent, 1972, p. 73.

11 *Ibid.*, pp. 116–17.

12 *Ibid.*, p. 75.

13 *Ibid.*, p. 135.

14 On this see Joel Feinberg, *Rights, Justice and the Bounds of Liberty: essays in social philosophy*, Princeton University Press, 1980, pp. 69–109.

15 Mill, *Utilitarianism. . .*, p. 153.

16 See D. Z. Phillipps and H. O. Mounce, *Moral Practices*, London, Routledge & Kegan Paul, 1969, ch. 6; and Peter Winch, *Ethics and Action*, London, Routledge & Kegan Paul, 1972, ch. 10.

17 H. L. A. Hart, *Law, Liberty and Morality*, Oxford University Press, 1963.

18 P. Devlin, *The Enforcement of Morals*, Oxford University Press, 1965.

19 These 'disintegration theses' are well discussed in C. L. Ten's *Mill on Liberty*, Oxford, Clarendon Press, 1980, pp. 86–92.

20 *Utilitarianism. . .*, pp. 132–3.

21 *Ibid.*, p. 114.

22 *Ibid.*, p. 75.

23 *Ibid.*, p. 144.

24 Geoffrey Marshall, *Constitutional Theory*, Oxford, Clarendon Press, 1971, pp. 156–7.

25 H. J. McCloskey, *John Stuart Mill: a Critical Study*, London, Macmillan, 1971, pp. 119–20.

26 H. B. Acton, 'Introduction' to Mill, *Utilitarianism. . .*, pp. xx–xxi.

27 R. P. Wolff, *The Poverty of Liberalism*, Boston, Beacon Press, 1968, pp. 8–15.

28 I refer, of course, to Popper's defence of falsificationism in *The Logic of Scientific Discovery*, London, Hutchinson, 1959.

29 On this, see P. K. Feyerabend, *Against Method*, London, New Left Books, 1975, p. 48.

30 Mill, *Utilitarianism. . .*, p. 99.

31 *Ibid.*, p. 46.

32 *Ibid.*, p. 46.

33 *Ibid.*, p. 107.

34 *Ibid.*, p. 82.

35 *Ibid.*, p. 85.

36 *Ibid.*, p. 104.

VI MILL'S DOCTRINE OF LIBERTY: A REAPPRAISAL

1 I am indebted to Derek Parfit's 'Personal Identity', *Philosophical Review*, 1971, vol. lxxx, pp. 3–27, and to Bernard Williams's discussions of the scalar nature of personal identity in his 'Persons, Character and Morality' in his *Moral Luck*, Cambridge University

Press, 1981, pp. 1–19.

2 On this see R. Nozick, *Anarchy, State and Utopia*, Oxford, Black-well, 1974, pp. 32–33; and D. H. Regan's 'Justifications for Paternalism' in J. R. Pennock and J. W. Chapman (eds), *Nomos XV, Limits of Law*, New York, Lieber-Atherton, 1974.

3 Robert Nozick, *Philosophical Explanations*, Oxford, Clarendon Press, 1981.

4 See P. K. Feyerabend, *Philosophical Papers: volume 2, Problems of Empiricism*, Cambridge University Press, 1981, p. 70, note 10.

5 *Ibid.*, vol. 1, *Realism, Rationalism and Scientific Method*, p. 142.

6 *The Subjection of Women*, in Alice C. Rossi (ed.), *Essays on Sex Equality*, University of Chicago Press, 1970, pp. 236–7. Note Mill's similar reliance on common sense and introspection in another context: 'It can only be determined (if mankind desire nothing but pleasure) by practised self-consciousness and self-observation, assisted by observation of others', *Utilitarianism, On Liberty and Considerations on Representative Government*, London, Dent, 1972, p. 36.

7 Maurice Cowling, *Mill and Liberalism*, Cambridge University Press, 1963.

8 See Ronald Dworkin, *Taking Rights Seriously*, London, Duckworth, 1977, and Bruce Ackerman, *Social Justice in the Liberal State*, New Haven and London, Yale University Press, 1980, for different versions of the liberal ideal of neutrality.

9 *A System of Logic*, bk 6, ch. 10, sect. 5.

10 Richard Wollheim, 'John Stuart Mill and Isaiah Berlin: The Ends of Life and the Preliminaries of Morality' in *The Idea of Freedom*, Oxford University Press, 1979, p. 267.

11 *Ibid.*, p. 267.

12 *Utilitarianism. . .*, p. 165.

13 For an account of Mill's views on socialism, see my 'John Stuart Mill on the Theory of Property', in A. Parel and T. Flanagan (eds), *Theories of Property: Aristotle to the Present*, Waterloo, Ontario, Wilfred Laurier University Press, 1979, pp. 257–80.

14 For an example of this error, see Ellen Paul, *Moral Revolution and Political Science: The Demise of Laisser-Faire in Nineteenth Century British Political Economy*, Westport, Conn., Greenwood Press, 1979.

15 Alasdair Macintyre, *After Virtue*, London, Duckworth, 1981, pp. 61–2.

16 See, on this, Bernard Williams, 'Conflicts of Value' in *Moral Luck*, Cambridge University Press, 1981, pp. 71–82.

17 Richard Wollheim, *The Sheep and the Ceremony: the Leslie Stephen Lecture*, Cambridge University Press, 1979, pp. 32–3.

18 Bernard Williams, 'A Critique of Utilitarianism', in *Utilitarianism: for and against*, Cambridge University Press, 1973, p. 135.

19 Mill's Doctrine of Liberty, because it does not presuppose his theory of human progress, is not vulnerable to Michael Oakeshott's

criticism of Mill's general philosophy of politics. See Oakeshott's *Rationalism in Politics*, London, Methuen, 1962, p. 136.

20 J. S. Mill, *Autobiography*, ch. V, para. 17. The passage is found in Max Lerner (ed.), *Essential Works of J. S. Mill*, New York, Bantam Books, 1961, pp. 98–9.

INDEX

141

Honderich, Ted, 23, 25, 38, 131n, 133n, 134n
Hume, David, 28, 111, 112

individuality, 16, 44, 70-3, 79-82, 113

Joseph, H.W.B., 42
justice, 13, 25, 28, 33, 52, 67, 68

Kant, Immanuel, 55, 66, 78

legal moralism, 100, 102
liberty, 6, 14-18, 23, 47, 55, 111, 122, 125
liberty, doctrine of, 14-18, 45-7, 48, 57, 59, 66, 68, 73, 77, 83, 84, 87, 93; Mill's liberalism and, 119-25; Mill's philosophy and, 111-16; the science of society and, 116-19; utility of, 125-9
Liberty, Principle of, 1, 3-5, 7, 8, 9, 11, 14, 16, 22, 35, 38, 39, 47, 48, 53, 57-63, 65-8, 93, 94, 96, 116, 117
logic of practice, 19-20
Lucas, John, 8, 131n, 135n
Lyons, David, 24, 131n, 132n, 133n

Macauley, Thomas Babington, Lord, 83
McClosky, H.J., 106, 131n, 138n
Macintyre, Alasdair, 125, 139n
Marshall, Geoffrey, 106, 138
Mill, James, 30; *Analysis of the Phenomena of the Human Mind*, 42, 43, 134n
Mill, John Stuart: and Aristotle, 80-1; areas of thought, 107-10; choice-making, 82; coercion, 96, 101; compatibilist thesis, 112; concept of happiness, 44-6, 71-3, 87, 88-9, 111, 125-6; criticism of writings, 1-10; duty, 26, 27; empiricism of, 83, 112-13; freedom of expression, 103-10; governmental intervention, 61-3; higher pleasure, 70, 87, 88-9; indirect utilitarianism and, 12, 13, 16, 38-42, 46-7, 60, 111; intrinsic value, 113-14; language of tendencies, 30; liberalism of, 119-25; moral rules, 51; moralism, 97-103; paternalism, 90-7; as a perfectionist, 87-8; personal autonomy, 78;

philosophical psychology of, 17, 56, 116; pleasure and, 42-4; revisionary interpretation of, 10-14, 22, 38; right conduct, 28-9; and scientific knowledge, 83, 114; servitude, 93; social stability, 57, 121; socialism, 124; theory of individuality, 13, 44, 79-82; theory of justice, 13, 60; theory of knowledge, 114-16; theory of moral rights, 53-5, 59, 63-9, 97; utilitarian morality, 2, 8, 13, 25, 28, 34, 37-42, 113; utilitarian strategies, 68; value-pluralism, 126-7; view of human nature, 13, 15, 84-6, 111; view of progress, 85, 111, 119-20, 121, 123; vital interests, 50-3, 57, 59, 60; willing slavery, 94; worthiness and, 40-1; wrong conduct, 30-4, 35-6, 38; *see also* individual works
Moore, G.E., 8, 42
moral rights, 53-5, 59, 63, 67-8
morality, 13, 25, 39, 97-103
Mounce, H.O., 102, 138n

nobility, 99
Nozick, Robert, 8, 66, 113, 114, 131n, 133n, 136n, 139n

On Liberty, 3-4, 9, 14, 17, 18, 23, 25, 34, 48, 49, 50, 57, 60, 61, 62, 66, 70, 72, 78, 79, 80, 83, 85-6, 92, 96, 101-2, 106-7, 114-16, 123, 128, 129, 137n

paternalism, 90-7, 100, 113
Phillipps, D.Z., 102, 138n
pleasure, 25, 42-4, 84
positivism, 118, 119
Prichard, H.A., 24, 133
Principles of Political Economy, 62-3, 92, 95, 101, 136n
prudence, 13, 32, 40, 100
punishment, 28, 30, 33, 36, 100-1

Rawls, J., 65, 66, 87, 88, 113, 136n, 137n
Rees, John C., 49-51, 131n, 135n
Regan, D.H., 66, 136n, 137n
Remarks on Bentham's Philosophy, 42
Riesman, David, 76, 136
Rousseau, Jean-Jacques, 55, 76

International Library of Philosophy

Editor: Ted Honderich

(*Demy 8vo*)

Allen, R.E. (Ed.), **Studies in Plato's Metaphysics** *464 pp. 1965.*
Plato's 'Euthyphro' and the Earlier Theory of Forms *184 pp. 1970.*
Allen, R.E. and Furley, David J.(Eds.), **Studies in Presocratic Philosophy**
Vol.1: The Beginnings of Philosophy *326 pp. 1970.*
Vol. 11: Eleatics and Pluralists *448 pp. 1975.*
Armstrong, D.M., **Perception and the Physical World** *208 pp. 1961.*
A Materialist Theory of the Mind *376 pp. 1967.*
Bambrough, Renford (Ed.), **New Essays on Plato and Aristotle**
184 pp. 1965.
Barry, Brian, **Political Argument** *382 pp. 1965.*
Becker, Lawrence C., **On Justifying Moral Judgments** *212 pp. 1973.*
† Blum, Lawrence, **Friendship, Altruism and Morality** *256 pp. 1980.*
Bogen, James, **Wittgenstein's Philosophy of Language** *256 pp. 1972.*
Brentano, Franz, **The Foundation and Construction of Ethics** *398 pp. 1973*
The Origin of our Knowledge of Right and Wrong *184 pp. 1969.*
Psychology from an Empirical Standpoint *436 pp. 1973.*
Sensory and Noetic Consciousness *168 pp. 1981.*
Broad, C.D., **Lectures on Psychical Research** *462 pp. 1962.*
Crombie, I.M., **An Examination of Plato's Doctrine**
*Vol.'1:*Plato on Man and Society *408 pp. 1962.*
Vol. 11: Plato on Knowledge and Reality *584 pp. 1963.*
Dennett, D.C., **Content and Conciousness** *202 pp. 1969.*
Dretske, Fred I., **Seeing and Knowing** *270 pp. 1969.*
Ducasse, C.J., **Truth, Knowledge and Causation** *264 pp. 1969.*
Fann. K.T. (Ed.), **Symposium on J.L. Austin** *512 pp. 1969.*
Findlay, J.N., **Plato: The Written and Unwritten Doctrines** *498 pp. 1974.*
Flew, Anthony, **Hume's Philosophy of Belief** *296 pp. 1961.*
Glover, Jonathan, **Responsibility** *212 pp. 1970.*
Goldman, Lucien, **The Hidden God** *424 pp. 1964.*
Hamlyn, D.W., **Sensation and Perception** *222 pp. 1961.*
†*Hornsby, Jennifer, **Actions** *152 pp. 1980.*
Husserl, Edmund, **Logical Investigations** *Vol.1: 456 pp. Vol.11: 464 pp.1970.*
Körner, Stephan, **Experience and Theory** *272 pp. 1966.*
*Linsky, Leonard, **Referring** *152 pp. 1967.*
Mackenzie, Brian D., **Behaviourism and the Limits of Scientific Method**
208 pp. 1977.
†*Mackie, J.L., **Hume's Moral Theory** *176 pp. 1980.*
Merleau-Ponty, M., **Phenomenology of Perception** *488 pp. 1962.*
Naess, Arne, **Scepticism,** *176 pp. 1969.*
† Nelson, William, **On Justifying Democracy** *192 pp. 1980.*
† Newton-Smith, W.H., **The Structure of Time** *276 pp. 1980.*
Perelman, Chaim, **The Idea of Justice and the Problem of Argument**
224 pp. 1963.
†*Putnam, Hilary, **Meaning and the Moral Sciences** *156 pp.1978.(Paperback
1980).*
Sayre, Kenneth M., **Cybernetics and the Philosophy of Mind** *280 pp. 1976.*